Engaged

Building Intentional Partnerships With Families

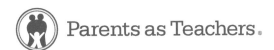
Parents as Teachers

Vision

■ All children will develop, learn and grow to realize their full potential.

Mission

■ Parents as Teachers promotes the optimal early development, learning and health of children by supporting and engaging their parents and caregivers.

Core Values

■ Parents are their children's first and most influential teachers.

■ The early years of a child's life are critical for optimal development and provide the foundation for success in school and life.

■ Established and emerging research should be the foundation of parent education and family support, curricula, training, materials and services.

■ All young children and their families deserve the same opportunities to succeed, regardless of any demographic, geographic or economic considerations.

■ An understanding and appreciation of the history and traditions of diverse cultures is essential in serving families.

Approach

■ The Parents as Teachers approach is to **partner**, **facilitate** and **reflect**. We do this at every level of our organization, from a parent educator visiting a family in their home, all the way to the work of the national center.

Published by:

Parents as Teachers National Center, Inc.
2228 Ball Drive, Saint Louis, Missouri 63146 USA
314.432.4330 • 866.PAT4YOU • FAX: 314.432.8963
info@ParentsAsTeachers.org
ParentsAsTeachers.org

ISBN 978-0-9904194-1-9

Preface

Because of the influence and impact of the work of teachers and early childhood professionals, conversations about child outcomes have historically focused on what happens within educational organizations. In recent decades, however, we have expanded our understanding of effective practices, and continue to learn that when families are actively engaged in their children's education, more children rise to their full potential.

Parents as Teachers core values are founded on the idea that parents are their children's first and most influential teachers. In order to reach our vision—that all children will develop, learn and grow to realize their full potential—families must be partners in this journey. Integral to our approach is the view that parent and family engagement is essential.

It is our hope that as you read *Engaged: Building Intentional Partnerships With Families,* you will discover a new lens through which you can examine family engagement within your organization. The research, reflections, examples, and values you will find in this book can provide a framework for deepening your practices, and for improving the quality of your relationships with families.

At Parents as Teachers, we have seen the positive impact when families are equal partners in their children's development and education, beginning at birth. We encourage you to continue to strive for this goal, through the challenges that might arise—including the discomfort that can come with good and necessary change.

We know you are working hard every day to ensure that each child is given the best opportunity to succeed, and we applaud your efforts. By continuing to invest the time, energy, and thought into effectively engaging families, you can empower staff, families, and the community to create the best possible outcomes for children.

Constance Gully, M.B.A., C.P.A.
President and Chief Executive Officer

Acknowledgments

President/Chief Executive Officer

Constance Gully, M.B.A., C.P.A.

Vice President of Professional and Program Development

Donna Hunt-O'Brien

Project Manager and Lead Writer

Lindsey Shah, M.S.W., L.C.S.W.

Contributing Editors

Amy De La Hunt, M.A.

Kelly McNerney, M.A., M.F.A.

Liz Talago

Tracy Cutchlow

Reviewers

Donna Hunt-O'Brien

Elanda Williams, M.A.

Kate McGilly, Ph.D.

Layout and Design Formatting

Amanda Million

Amy Luna

Erin Westfall

Madeline Haraway

Special Thanks

The writing of *Engaged: Building Intentional Partnerships With Families* was informed by many Parents as Teachers products, with our approach (partner, facilitate, and reflect) providing a backbone to the work. We would like to thank all of the individuals who have informed the content by sharing your stories and providing us with research to help spread the work of family engagement. A special thanks to Parents as Teachers National Center staff who came together to share their vast experiences with us, and the host and guests of our podcast *Intentional Partnerships*, produced in collaboration with Strong Fathers-Strong Families.

- Mike Hall
- Renea Butler-King
- Donna Kosicki
- Jill Spillman
- Christina Hodgkinson
- Vito Borrello
- Salvador Romero

- Matt Arend
- Christy and Ed Roberts
- Karla Kush
- Yolanda Chapple Munson
- Loretta Miles
- Marina Montoya

A Note to Readers

Many of the ancedotes and personal stories found throughout the book come from an anonymous family engagement survey conducted by Parents as Teachers in 2018, in addition to personal communications, and are not cited in the Notes section.

Table of Contents

Engaged

Introduction

No matter your profession, you've probably heard the truism that "it takes a village to raise a child" more times than you can count. This saying, though perhaps cliché, contains a large kernel of truth—one that people who work with children understand deeply. Each of you reading this book is a part of that village, part of the team that is working together with families towards a common goal: to support children in growing to reach their full potential.

Anyone who works with children is also likely to be keenly aware of the fact that children do not grow, learn, or interact with organizations in a vacuum. Their families are a constant presence in their lives, influencing not only the direction of their growth and development, but every step along their path.

Families influence all of the spaces where children spend their days—including the organization in which you interact with children—whether you are a teacher, school administrator, home visitor, health care provider, family support staff, or one of the many other professionals that impact children.

A growing body of research confirms that, in order to do this work to the best of our abilities, we need to walk in partnership with families, and acknowledge the enormous roles that families play in children's lives. Harnessing the power of families through family engagement moves all parties closer towards the goals we share for children.

What do we mean by family engagement?

Definitions

Merriam-Webster defines family as the foundational social unit. Often a family is defined as the people related to a child by blood, or designated caregivers who have responsibility for a child—and they are endlessly diverse. Many children are being raised by grandparents, aunts, uncles, siblings, and other supportive adults. Even when these adults are not the primary caregivers of a child, they often play active roles in the child's life. They may be picking up and dropping off children from school or activities, or they may be the main points of contact while mom and dad work. They may be helping with homework or emotionally supporting children. Each of these roles influences the overall growth and development of the child, and all are included in our conversation when talking about engaging the family. We can partner with everyone who is engaged in the child's life as an active player.

Parents as Teachers defines family engagement as an intentional, ongoing partnership to which all parties contribute. These partners include parents, organizations, and community members who work together to plan, develop, and evaluate activities and programs that promote parenting growth, as well as children's development, learning, and wellness.

In 2013, the U.S. Department of Education, in collaboration with SEDL researchers Karen Mapp and Paul Kuttner, published what is perhaps the most well-known framework for family engagement, *Partners in Education: A Dual Capacity-Building Framework for Family-School Partnerships*. This framework is widely available, and it is often referred to by organizations and schools as they explore their own process of defining what family engagement means to them.

In 2018, an update was published to the original definition of family engagement included in the framework. This new version defines family engagement as "a full, equal, and equitable partnership among families, educators, and community partners to promote children's learning and development from birth through college and career." (Apart from the revised definition, the complete framework update was not yet available when this book went to press).

Of course, there are many other definitions and frameworks for family engagement, and one may ring truer with you than others. They might be useful as you either begin to explore or refine your own definition.

Agreeing on what family engagement means to you and the community you serve is an important starting point. This book is designed to help you navigate that conversation—shaped by values that form the foundation of successful engagement.

The family engagement continuum

It is useful to think of the ever-evolving process of family engagement as a continuum, rather than a destination. Researcher Anne Henderson and illustrator Bob Dahm were among the first to depict this continuum's defining characteristics. At one end of the spectrum, there is no partnership with families whatsoever. Parents drop their children off and pick them up with little or no interaction or voice as to what happens within the organization. What used to be called "parent involvement" falls somewhere in the middle; families are invited to participate but, more often than not, this means doing things that benefit the professional or teacher, such as sorting papers, raising funds, or decorating a classroom. On the other end—the "partnership" end of the continuum—parents and caregivers are truly engaged with staff, and everyone works together to reach the best outcomes for children.

The reality is that many of our partnerships with families lie somewhere in between the two ends of this continuum. Some days it might feel closer to one end than the other, and that is OK. In addition, each individual family and staff member also falls somewhere along the continuum, influenced by who they are interacting with, their own past experiences, and many other factors.

The complex layers of successful family engagement contribute to movement back and forth along the continuum; our placement within it is seldom static. Although this can make it challenging to gauge progress and measure milestones, it's also a wonderful opportunity in the sense that no setback is ever permanent.

Outcomes

Benefits to children

There is a growing body of research that demonstrates all kinds of positive outcomes that result from children being surrounded by families that are engaged in their learning from an early age. While the findings on strong family engagement tend to be relatively recent, and somewhat difficult to quantify, what has been discovered are broad impacts. Compellingly, we are learning that while children with more engaged families are more successful by traditional academic measures, they are showing positive gains in many other areas as well.

Educator and author Janis Keyser notes that when children are exposed to healthy partnerships and relationships between the adults around them, they are more likely to develop those types of relationships themselves. Children will learn to partner, collaborate, communicate, and more—just by watching how the adults around them do these things. For example, in educational settings, the relationships students see between their teachers and their parents play a significant role in how they will eventually build these relationships themselves; both in the short term with their current teachers, and later on, when they have children of their own. Moreover, children are much more likely to feel safe when they know that their parents trust the adults with whom they spend the majority of their days.

"Since the U.S. Department of Education issued the 1994 report on *Strong Families, Strong Schools,* the body of evidence showing that family engagement impacts learning has continued to grow. Schools that engage families find that their students have higher grades, show faster rates of literacy acquisition, attend school more regularly, and are more likely to graduate."

– Panorama Education, *Reducing Barriers to Family Engagement*

Benefits to families

Children are not the only ones to benefit from family engagement efforts. In *Ripples of Transformation,* Melia Franklin divides benefits to families into three areas:

- Increasing positive parenting behaviors within the home

- Shaping programs and services in the community

- Influencing policies as an advocate in larger systems

In each of these realms, families who have experienced engagement as partners demonstrate a noticeable shift in confidence. Enhancing parenting capacity and improving parent-child relationships is our focus at Parents as Teachers. Our home-visiting model has demonstrated that when children's families are engaged in their early learning and development, they often experience a kind of "virtuous cycle" of positive outcomes. In partnership with parent educators, parent's knowledge of their child's learning and development increases, and they grow more aware of their parenting abilities. As noted in the *Family Engagement Inventory,* as parents' awareness of their abilities grows, they begin to attend events that increase their exposure to diverse people and parenting strategies, causing this awareness to continue to develop. Parents are then more likely to be involved with learning activities in the home, and are more involved in their child's education. They feel a greater sense of belonging in the larger community, and have more opportunities to network with other families and service providers. Although Parents as Teachers focuses on increasing positive parenting behaviors during the earliest years of children's lives, family engagement is shown to influence parenting practices later in children's educational journeys as well.

Families' voices are critical to the development and maintenance of quality programs. When invited, parents—especially those who have built confidence as leaders in their home—may lend their strengths, ideas, and support to a program or service.

Moreover, experts at the Annenberg Institute have found that many parents empowered through engagement efforts are drawn to civic action, both at local and national levels. The United Parent Leaders Action Network, or UPLAN, is just one example of an organization founded by parent leaders who sought a national forum for sharing ideas and organizing around educational policy issues. Parent-led organizations such as UPLAN are shaping education for children from birth through college.

Each family will be impacted in its own way. Wherever and however they engage, families can benefit from increased confidence in their role as parents. This confidence may not necessarily push them towards civic action, but it can strengthen their capacity to better understand, interact with, and influence the programming in which their children participate.

Benefits to staff and organizations

Parent educators, family support professionals, and educators may find that their days get a little easier as they embark on their own partnering journeys with families. The *Family Engagement Inventory* notes that they are likely to have higher morale, deeper understanding of students' home cultures, and more avenues for communication about both positive and challenging issues.

The Administration for Children and Families finds that outcomes at the organizational level may include improved quality of programs and services, better academic student outcomes, decreased behavior problems, higher attendance rates, and increased satisfaction among families.

Having a comprehensive family engagement strategy across an organization can:

- Facilitate communication with parents.
- Create a network of support around children in all spaces.
- Reduce the time spent trying to establish or maintain communication between staff and families.
- Reduce the stress staff might feel when talking to parents.
- Provide access to resources and tools to which they would not otherwise have access.

These are only a few of the possible benefits! Ultimately, empowering professionals to partner with families can make them feel more satisfied and competent in their roles, and provide them with the intrinsic satisfaction that they are more effectively contributing to children's success. Depending on your organization, staff members may not be familiar with the benefits of family engagement practices. For instance, teachers are rarely given explicit guidance on family engagement during teacher training programs, and family engagement remains unfamiliar territory. By providing staff in your organization more opportunities to learn and practice their engagement skills, you are providing them with access to previously untapped resources.

Benefits to communities

Increased family engagement promotes positive relationships throughout communities. Since communities are made up of families and organizations, it is no surprise that what benefits the individuals within a community also contributes to the well-being of the community as a whole. Research included in the *Family Engagement Inventory* shows a strong link between family engagement practices and positive community outcomes, such as higher numbers of community members reporting trusting relationships with each other. The research also shows positive correlations in relation to juvenile justice systems; for example, there were lower cases of recidivism in communities where family engagement strategies were being effectively implemented.

As mentioned in the previous section on benefits to families, parent advocacy also grows out of family engagement. The Annenberg Institute reports that parent advocates can raise awareness of important policy implications among legislators, expand funding opportunities, improve standards for care and services, and help shape plans for systemic reform. When families are given a voice and space to participate meaningfully in their children's education, they may go on to engage as an advocate for the benefit of the entire community.

What this book is (and is not)

Parents as Teachers has been working since its conception to empower families by improving their knowledge of their child's development and strengthening their parenting skills. Working to deepen engagement of families in home visits, group connections, and community resources has been, and continues to be, a critical part of the work that our organization does.

We are not alone in this effort. Over the last decade or so, many individuals—from professionals on the ground, to leaders in the Federal Government—have spent a great deal of time and energy trying to figure out what leads to successful family engagement. There are conferences dedicated to sharing promising practices and evidence-based strategies, and there are national organizations working to create a cohesive set of policies and standards at the state and federal levels. Leading entities, like the U.S. Department of Education, have put resources towards research, and are supporting implementation at the local level.

While researching for this book, we gathered countless stories from people all over the country—the voices of professionals in teaching, administration, early childhood, home visiting, and more. We uncovered research and numerous resources including activities designed to improve family engagement. The phenomenal wealth of information and strategies that we identified was both exciting and overwhelming.

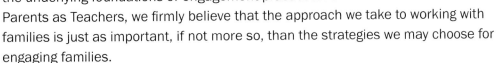

We started to ask ourselves: If all of these thoughtful, research-backed and experience-informed strategies already exist, why are so many organizations and individuals still struggling to engage families?

The exploration of this question led us to take a step back, to look at what happens before the strategies, at the underlying foundations of engagement practices. At Parents as Teachers, we firmly believe that the approach we take to working with families is just as important, if not more so, than the strategies we may choose for engaging families.

With the best of intentions, organizations and professionals set out to improve their family engagement plans; they might tackle this by compiling a list of strategies they would like to employ, and then diving head first into their action plan. What this book asks, and offers, is the time to take that step back—*before* diving into strategies—to reflect on family engagement and the lens through which we view the roles of our organizations and families.

What we are exploring in this book are the deeper, foundational questions that need to be addressed prior to choosing effective engagement tools. For this reason, you will not find a list of strategies to engage families—you can find these included in many high-quality resources that already exist. Though you will read anecdotes that highlight some specific ways that professionals in the field are doing this work, the focus of these pages is on the conversations and self-exploration that can happen before choosing any particular strategies. We believe this approach can help avoid common pitfalls, identify potential blind spots, and build a solid jumping-off point. We hope to guide you into deeper conversations about the beliefs and perspectives that your organization— and you personally—may hold. By delving into these conversations, you will discover ways to implement strategies that are an authentic fit for your organization and the community you serve.

Each of you works incredibly hard every day to build connections and promote the health, well-being, and development of children. We know that you are walking side by side with families on this journey, to the best of your ability. Sometimes it is working beautifully— connections are secure, and relationships are growing. In other places, it might be more of a struggle. You may find yourself at a crossroads, not really knowing where to go next.

This book explores a variety of scenarios and challenges you're likely to encounter. It is meant to support your journey into intentional engagement. It is also intended to help you to identify where the gaps may exist in your current family engagement plan. It can serve as a guide as you start, or continue, to have real conversations about why things are, or are not, working. It can help you dig deeper into engaging every family.

This book is divided into 10 chapters, each highlighting a value that we believe is instrumental in shaping the foundation of effective family engagement. These chapters include research and data, stories and examples from the field, and reflections that can support you. They may also provide you with an additional lens to look through, as you examine how each of the values lives within (or is missing from) your partnerships with families.

At Parents as Teachers, we work primarily with families of young children, but have drawn from many disciplines while researching for this book; many emerging best practices in family engagement come from, and are applicable to, multiple

The values we'll explore

- Trust
- Respect
- Responsibility
- Generosity
- Accessibility

- Integration
- Compassion
- Initiative
- Persistence
- Sustainability

fields. We share the belief that establishing patterns and consistency in how we engage families across sectors can support everyone in this work.

Family engagement can be difficult. It takes time and resources to make it work. Like most things worth doing, it isn't easy. Wherever you, your organization, and the parents you partner with may be on the engagement continuum, there is room for growth. We hope this book is one resource that can help support you on your journey. This book, and the values within it, are intended to help you develop as a professional and grow as an organization in ways that will enhance what you do every day to engage families at a deeper level.

As we all grapple with the challenges of engaging families, we can learn so much from each other! In the end, we are all working towards the same goal: we all want the best for children.

A strengths-based approach

Families have incredible resources and strengths—not to mention the fact that they are the most knowledgeable sources of information about their child. As the Center for the Study of Social Policy points out, families' expertise deserves to be recognized when they interact with the professionals who support them. While this is not new information, this starting point may represent a shift in how some educators, service providers, and early childhood organizations approach their work.

Strengths-based vs. Deficit Approach

The Child Welfare Information Gateway provides one way to think about a strengths-based approach. They define it as "...policies, practice methods, and strategies that identify and draw upon the strengths of children, families, and communities. Strengths-based practice involves a shift from a deficit approach, which emphasizes problems and pathology, to a positive partnership with the family." They also report that, "a family-centered, strengths-based approach is associated with increased service engagement, increased parenting competency, and enhanced interaction among family members.

Strengths-based approaches are built into the training that many of us have experienced, and are woven into the practices that we have absorbed in our professional development. While we can often see the wisdom in an approach that focuses on strengths, the language we use and the actions we take each day within our organizations and schools do not always reflect a strengths-based framework.

It is important to take a step back every once in a while, to dive back into the theories that inform our approach, and to remind ourselves what we really mean when we say we take a strengths-based approach to our work. At Parents as Teachers, the different strategies we encourage parent educators to employ—to empower and promote autonomy for parents—are most effective when parent educators believe in the parents' capacity to find their own answers and build their own skills.

Building sustainable practices with families—whether at a school, in a community organization, or in their own homes—becomes much easier when they are built upon the strengths that the families already have within them. Building on your families' strengths can also push efforts further and faster as they are driven by the skills, values, and interests of those in the community.

Despite our best intentions, we can slip into a deficit approach at times, and focus our work on identifying families' weaknesses instead of building on strengths. Many psychologists have argued that humans are hard-wired to focus on what we perceive as problems, due to what is referred to as our "negativity bias." An article published in the *General Review of Psychology*, "Bad is Stronger Than Good", concluded that, "in general, and apart from a few carefully crafted exceptions, negative information receives more processing and contributes more strongly to the final impression than does positive information." As we become more aware of the tendency to focus on the negative aspects over the positive, we can also become more intentional about renewing our commitments to a strengths-based approach.

The truth is that no partnership can be successful if either side sees the other as incapable. A recognition of knowledge and skills on all sides of the partnership can help things move smoothly and can move the whole group forward. Many authors and theorists agree that equipping everyone to influence decisions and demonstrate self-efficacy empowers the entire group.

The ideas within each of the chapters of this book have been informed by, and formulated with, a focus on maintaining a strengths-based approach to family engagement work. The strengths-based lens forms a large part of the foundation and approach we hope will become an intentional and integral part of your own family engagement strategies.

"Families are children's first and most important teachers, advocates, and nurturers. As such, strong family engagement is central—not supplemental—to promoting children's healthy development and wellness."

– U.S. Department of Health and Human Services and U.S. Department of Education, *Policy Statement on Family Engagement*

Relationships and partnerships

At the heart of the research and shared experience on engagement, there is one common thread: relationships. This shouldn't come as a surprise to anyone who has worked with families or children. After all, families themselves are complex systems where relationships are central. Families interact with a whole spectrum of service-delivery organizations around their child's education and development,

 and they need to be able to trust that those educators and providers care about their child's growth, health, and well-being. Staff in these organizations also need to be able to trust that families will be invaluable partners in the process of achieving the best outcomes for children. Authors of *Developmental Parenting: A Guide for Early Childhood Practitioners* note that the relationships that you build with families, and the partnerships that result from those relationships, are the most critical components of family engagement. Engaging families in their child's education and well-being is easiest when you have a consistent, mutually respectful relationship.

Shifting from a service-oriented relationship to a partnership-focused relationship can be challenging, especially if you or others have been in the field for a while. Sometimes changing habits is more difficult than developing new practices. While partnership has always been a topic of discussion in education and early childhood, we are beginning to define what partnering means with a little more clarity, and a little more depth.

An ideal partnership exists when both sides bring what they have to the table, in terms of expertise and knowledge, and are willing to learn from each other and work together. We know that in practice, partnerships aren't always ideal. When we talk about partnering with families in this book, we acknowledge that some partnerships are a bit off-balance—there may be little contribution from one party and a lot from the other. Some days may look less like partnering and more like leading from one side or the other. It's our hope that you do not abandon the effort, and that this book will help you begin the work of evening out imbalances.

As an organization, it can be helpful to think about what it means to you to truly partner with families, especially when challenges arise. Being clear about expectations—both your own and those of families—can support you and your colleagues as you strive toward deepening relationships.

Conversations about expectations and what partnership means to each party can also be a great starting point for dialogue about engagement with families. Just as you have internal expectations, families also have ideas about what to expect and what will be expected of them as partners.

Being in true partnership with families is a worthy goal to strive for—one that takes a lot of work, with plenty of trial and error along the way. You may find that some families feel easier to partner with than others. Families that initiate a relationship, and are eager to partner with you, are a natural place to start, but don't forget they are not the only ones. We challenge you to embrace those families, and to keep growing with those that don't feel as easy to engage. There are endless possibilities that are waiting in the partnerships with families that you might not have anticipated—and they can be infinitely rewarding!

"In too many cases, family engagement efforts begin with policy makers, researchers, and professionals determining what families need to do, and then developing messages that will generate "buy-in," support, and participation. They treat parents as consumers, who must be "sold" an agenda in order to be successful in achieving their goals."

– Don't Forget the Families: The Missing Piece in America's Effort to Help All Children Succeed

Roles in Partnerships

More than two decades ago, Lilian Katz, an international leader in early childhood education, explained the idea of partnership by highlighting ways in which the roles of parents and teachers are unique. They each make different but complimentary contributions to a child's learning and growth. Katz argued that it is ultimately the responsibility of programs to support, but not replace, parents' own goals and patterns of responding to their children.

Reflecting on the values of family engagement

During our research and conversations with families and professionals, we found that the values we've selected and highlighted kept coming to the forefront.

Although identified, we struggled to isolate values and peel them apart; how can one separate respect from trust, trust from persistence, or persistence from responsibility? The stories of success or failure we investigated were not confined to one specific value that was key to—or detracted from—their success. While we divided the book into these chapters to make the concepts easier to process, the web of these values ran through each and every example we found. We know, too, that this web of values is a more realistic picture of the reality of the work that is being done. Nevertheless, it is our hope that you can look to each of the examples provided in the chapters, to see the individual values highlighted, as well as the layers of each value that exists within. Ultimately, we believe each of the values we've included is an essential component of family engagement.

The purpose of the following chapters is to allow us to go deeper—underneath strategies—to examine the principles and relationships that form the basis of authentic family engagement. In any line of work, it is important to remember who we share common interests and goals with, and whose well-being and success is tied with our own. It is important to zoom-out and examine the lens through which we understand family engagement in our organizations, and to take the time to reflect on the values that inform that effort. In many organizations, family engagement remains an under-utilized practice that has the capacity to truly bring about important changes.

We know that by developing a strong and intentional family engagement framework that organizations, families, and communities will move towards the shared outcomes and goals that benefit everyone, especially children.

Trust

Relationships are reciprocal. Families need to trust staff, staff needs to trust families, and programs need to trust each other. Without trust, relationships fall apart, or, at the very least, they may exist but not be genuine. Establishing a groundwork of trust is a necessary first step to productive, meaningful partnerships.

Trust is the foundation of any good relationship; this is especially true for relationships between organizations and the families they serve. Trust is often built as part of a quiet, behind-the-scenes process. Sometimes this process is organized and voluntary, and both sides agree to work together to build trust. This may happen, for example, when a family first enters a new setting, such as a new school or child care center. However, in some situations, families are involuntary participants in services, such as when a family is referred for special services or therapy as part of an early intervention program, and is unsure of the process. Trust can be built in these types of situations too, but research presented by the Search Institute shows that it could take three times as long.

Of course, trust does not develop in isolation, or over the course of a single day. Experts at the Federal Government's Institute of Educational Sciences note that, "trust is built over time, based on interactions that occur on a daily basis and with consistent behavior from both sides. If families and educators do not have experience interacting with one another, then they may rely on the other person's reputation and on something they have in common, such as race, gender, age, religion, or upbringing."

Because we often base trust on the factors that we have in common, when we have very little or nothing in common it can take much longer for trust to develop. Intentionally seeking out and creating spaces for people to have face-to-face interactions and build relationships offers opportunities to build trust much more quickly.

It's likely that your organization or school is already intentionally seeking out and frequently communicating with families, but the topics we communicate about matter as well. When we call families just to deliver or obtain information, it does not leave much room for building the types of relationships that strengthen trust. Getting to know each other personally provides space to learn about what we have in common; this is how we begin to develop and deepen trust.

For Salvador Romero, Coordinator of Family and Community Engagement in his West Virginia school district, trust and relationships are practically synonymous. Romero takes every opportunity to talk to families when he's out in the community, to get to know who they are as people, and as parents. Sometimes they call his cell phone—and he's OK with that, even if they happened to get his number years ago, back in his days as an administrator in the school. "That is where I get the most valuable feedback," Romero explains. "If there is something going on that they are not happy with, or that they have concerns about, they are not shy to let me know. Because we do have that relationship, that trust, which is really critical in the work that we do." As Romero makes clear, in order to receive that family feedback a relationship based on mutual trust has to be established first.

Trust – what is it?

The topic of trust in educational settings is not a new one. In *Trust Matters: Leadership for Successful Schools*, Megan Tschannen-Moran offers five key components that are necessary for building trust:

1. **Benevolence**—There is a sense that the other person cares about your well-being

2. **Reliability**—You have confidence that the person will come through

3. **Competence**—You believe the person can do what they say they will

4. **Honesty**—You experience an authentic interaction that has integrity

5. **Openness**—The person fully shares relevant information

Trust through transitions

From a very early age, children are aware of their own relationships—and their families' relationships—with the professionals around them. Children are attuned to whether or not they, and their parents, feel wanted within the professional space. They notice when trust grows or declines.

Many structural changes take place when students transition from preschool and early childhood education settings into kindergarten. The classroom itself, and the child's experience in it, becomes more structured to fit the day of older elementary school children; this creates a perception that the elementary or kindergarten classroom is a less flexible place for families to engage with teachers, and is a space more focused on structured student learning. There is often only one teacher in kindergarten (possibly assisted by an aide) and the ratio of students to teacher becomes much higher.

In terms of the level of communication with families compared with early childhood settings, there is a clear burden on teachers as they have more families to talk with, and less time to do so. Because there is such limited time in kindergarten and beyond, it is important to reflect on the intention behind each interaction. Maybe there truly isn't sufficient time to engage deeply with families. If this is the case, how are the current communication opportunities maximized in order to build relationships within the time constraints?

Renea Butler-King, a social worker in Oklahoma who has spent years observing classrooms, sees many examples of this decline in trust-building interactions between early education and elementary schools. "Within an early childhood program, be it a Head Start program, be it an in-home program, the whole family is welcome. But somewhere around age three or four, when we are trying to get children ready for public school, we start disconnecting from family. They are no longer welcomed the same way," she explains.

Developmentally, preschoolers are hard-wired to pay attention to differences. They take note of this change from their preschool to their elementary school and start to think that if it's not safe for their family, it's not going to be safe for them. "And so," Butler-King continues, "we start to have some challenges with behavior, and then the school system doesn't quite know how to go back and reengage that welcoming piece."

Fortunately, building trust and relationships is a great way to begin to support children in overcoming or reversing those challenging behavioral trends. Just as children are watching to see if you and the people they care about aren't connecting, they also are carefully watching to see when you are. If children believe that their parents trust the teacher, and can see that the teacher respects the parents, children will act differently. As researcher and author Ann Ishimaru notes, simply having a relationship with families is not enough to build trust. A relationship is just a structure with possibility.

So how do we negotiate the limits and constraints of time and school structures so that we can still prioritize trust and trust building with families? If children are picking up on the differences when they transition to a new classroom or environment, how can we show them the reciprocated efforts to communicate and build trust with families, even if we don't have the kind of time we'd like to dedicate to these interactions?

Despite time constraints, there are many ways that professionals can interact with children and families to demonstrate efforts to build trust. For example, acknowledging families when they come into the building or room, by saying hello and genuinely asking how they are, demonstrates to children that you care. Using relaxed, friendly body language and a warm tone of voice in your small, day-to-day interactions with families lays a foundation for the positive relationships that become successful partnerships.

Importance of trust between children and educators

Establishing trust with families is one of many factors to consider when looking at behavior in children—but it can often be overlooked, as it may not be the most obvious factor. Another often underestimated factor when looking at children's behavior, particularly through transitions, is the trust that exists between the child and the provider or educator. Whether or not a child trusts the teacher or staff not only influences how the child behaves, but also impacts whether or not the family will trust you.

Building trusting relationships with children takes time and effort. We should not assume that just because a child is in our classroom they therefore trust us, or believe that we respect them. Taking the time to build that relationship can be powerful in shifting the dynamic, both inside of the classroom and with families.

Trust and respect

Research also tells us that there is an important relationship between trust and respect, and that when students and families feel respected, they are more willing to trust the organization or school. For example, one parent who was interviewed—the mother of a child with special needs—noted that the respect that each staff member gave to her child was critical in her decision to trust that staff member. Making this connection between respect and trust can prompt front-line individuals to think about ways to intentionally leverage their relationships with children in order to improve rapport with their families. Paying attention to the small ways in which respect for the child is demonstrated—for example, though positive feedback and rapport-building conversations—can pay huge dividends in terms of building trust with families too.

Additional strategies that can be used to demonstrate respect for the child, grounded in strengths-based theories, include:

- Sending monthly or bi-monthly postcards with an accomplishment or strength of the child

- Seeking to understand the meaning behind a behavior

- Providing staff training on ways to encourage positive behavior

- Tracking behaviors with data, and providing accurate feedback to families

- Having collaborative, proactive conversations with parents regarding behavior shifts when they begin, as opposed to waiting or delaying

If strengths-based practices and strategies for building trust with families are not embedded in the day-to-day practices and policies of your organization it may be challenging to shift behaviors in staff. It's helpful to have administration set policies and expectations for staff around interactions with families that can improve trust between the school and the families. This shift can be challenging because though we might think that we are acting through a strengths-based lens, in reality, our practices may stray from the ideal.

In addition to setting policies, modeling strengths-based strategies that can be used with families and children can be a useful practice, as staff members begin to adjust their own attitudes and behaviors. Identify individuals who have established trusting relationships with families, and look to see what is working for them; encourage them to share with colleagues and offer suggestions that have been helpful to them in building trust and relationships with families.

How do your verbal and non-verbal interactions with parents demonstrate mutual trust to the child?

Can you think of a staff member who is particularly effective or helpful in building trust with families?

How can you support other staff in replicating that behavior?

Regaining trust

Research and experience—both our own and those of the people we have spoken with—highlight a lack of trust as one of the major barriers to successful engagement. Author Charles Feltman explains that by "lack of trust," families often are referring to a feeling that something they value (such as their child) is not safe with a person or organization. When the bond of trust is broken, one partner is less likely to risk becoming vulnerable to the other partner's actions. When either side of a partnership is not willing to be vulnerable, growth in the relationship can prove to be a real challenge.

"A focus on relationship building is especially important in circumstances where there has been a history of mistrust between families and school or district staff."

– Karen L. Mapp and Paul J. Kuttner, *Partners in Education*

Distrust

Trust or distrust is not often based on an individual's relationship with another specific person, but rather on perceptions about the institution or organization being represented. For example, all families have an idea of what "school" means to them. They may trust schools in general because of positive experiences, or they may distrust schools in general because past experiences stir up negative emotions. Yet another option: families may trust schools in general, but not the specific school where they had a bad experience. The same goes for families' ideas of teachers, home visitors, or any other service organization or professional.

What follows is that much of the work you may find yourself doing to regain trust might not have anything to do with you personally, or your past interactions at all! Each interaction you have with a family is filtered through their previous experiences, for good or bad. This can complicate the process. You may not be exactly sure where that trust was broken, or why—and the family may not be able to articulate that either. Don't be hung up on your desire to right past wrongs. Instead, intentionally demonstrate, over and over, in big ways and in small, that this family can trust you and your organization going forward.

While setting new relationship expectations and moving forward are important for building trust, acknowledging and validating past wrongs may also be a necessary step before you can move forward. Even if those past wrongs were not related to, or a result of, your own actions, this conversation can support actions that say: "I hear you, I understand why this is difficult for you, and we will work together to make sure it doesn't happen again."

These conversations are especially critical if the negative interactions in the past did involve your personal relationship with the family. It can be difficult to have these conversations, but it can be even more difficult, if not impossible, to move forward without acknowledging these realities as well. An important step in these situations is not only to acknowledge past harm, but also to see if there is a measure of accountability that needs to be taken—in the form of owning responsibility, or even making amends—for past missteps. Of course, this is helpful practice in all relationships, but can go a long way in terms of establishing trust with families. It is important to clear the past and emphasize that you'd like to turn over a new page with parents—not allow past conflict to dominate the interactions with the family moving forward. These conversations in and of themselves are a way to begin to build trust with families.

Creating a shared vision

In a perfect world, we would always be able to resolve past conflicts, and move forward with a clean slate, in agreement with everyone. The real world tends to be more complicated. At times, working with families, we may simply not be able to find common ground, or reach a point where a conflict feels totally resolved or "fixed."

In her book, *Braving the Wilderness: The Quest for True Belonging and the Courage to Stand Alone*, research professor and author Brené Brown suggests transforming a disagreement by shifting the focus from what happened in the past to what is happening now. It's important to note that this does not mean refusing to acknowledge or talk about the past. This shift from what happened to what is happening occurs after acknowledging and validating past wrongs. After shifting the focus to the present, move forward and create an opportunity for connection, shifting again to what the partners are trying to accomplish in the future. Even in situations where the two sides disagree on strategies, if they can agree on a shared vision, they may be able to transform their relationship into one of optimism and trust.

For most of us, this shared vision is centered on moving towards success. When the going gets rough, taking a step back to refocus on the child—what your shared goals are for his or her future—can help both sides clarify why they are making choices they are. Be cautious to ensure that the goals are shared goals; reframing in the context of the goals of just one side can have the opposite effect, creating division.

Moving forward

Relationship experts at the Gottman Institute recognize that it can be hard to reconnect after trust has been broken. "Rebuilding trust requires a consistent and dependable energy of acceptance and respect." At times organizations might be inclined to "pursue" families in order to try to demonstrate trustworthiness; this can sometimes take the form of pressuring families to engage in new activities by reaching out through too many phone calls, emails, flyers, and so on. However, offering reassurance—rather than pursuit—is a better way to restore the essential element of trust between family engagement partners. Continue to show a family that they can trust you in the interactions you are already having. These may be small gestures, but they will build trust more quickly than if someone is being chased down and repeatedly asked to participate in things, so that you can prove they can trust you.

Opportunities to build trust happen in every interaction with families, both intentional and unintentional. Something as small as how people are greeted when they walk in the door can support the building of trust or the destruction of it. In fact, these small, unscripted moments can be just as critical to the foundation of trust as the intentional engagement opportunities that organizations create.

Think about all of the organic moments you have with families that feel genuine to you. You may notice that they include a multitude of different interactions, and that they fit each family's preferences and needs. These positive interactions support families as they move through the process of engaging. Letting families know how important these moments are to you reinforces the fact that the organization operates from a baseline of positive interaction, and that you are intentional about rebuilding trust.

reflection

What experiences might families in your community have had that impact their level of trust in certain institutions?

What do you do to prevent negative past experiences from affecting present interactions?

We know it's important... so how do we do it?

We may be able to see that trust is the key to developing productive relationships with families, but we may not always know how, when, or where to begin building that trust. What are the actions that we can take to show families that our organizations are trustworthy? How can we assure parents and communities that we will value the trust they offer us, not endanger it? As with all relationships, what matters most is what we do. Taking actions that foster and preserve trust will go a long way in working towards building the types of relationships we would like to have with families.

"Trust promotes dialogue; the more reciprocal the dialogue, the more awareness is fostered."

– **Student Achievement Division**, *Ontario Capacity Building Series*

Honest conversations

As trust deepens between parties, relationships are able to deepen and prosper, too. Open dialogues—focused on something other than the child's behavior or grades—create space for families and staff to truly get to know each other, to understand how to develop a partnership that can support their children in growing and prospering.

While this does not mean these relationships are always easy or smooth, it does mean that these relationships can form a foundation that helps partners to be productive, despite disagreements. Open and honest conversations can reveal both strengths and divisions in the room, both of which are necessary to address in order to move forward. When organizations and families trust each other, they allow each other to make mistakes, and trust that attempts to support each other through these shortcomings will be well received. These open and trusting relationships support families and organizations navigating the challenges that come with raising thriving young children.

Parent cafés: In these facilitated conversations, families, family engagement professionals, and organizational staff (or any combination of these) gather and give each other permission to speak freely within a safe space. The structure of the café supports initial dialogue around topics provided by facilitators—usually lighter and less threatening in nature—in order to build the relationships that can withstand tougher conversations. Look to Strengthening Families™ for more information on their Parent Cafés.

Parent-provider cafés: These events often engage families by first inviting parents into the planning and formulation of group and classroom content. Following the planning sessions are guided conversations that emphasize active listening and mindfulness when talking about optimal child development. This model is derived from the World Café model, via Zero to Three, in partnership with the Minnesota Department of Human Services. They've found that a collaborative planning process is one of the keys to success because it draws participants to engage ahead of time, and ensures smooth functioning during the café.

Open-ended questions: The Right Question Institute teaches the skill of asking good questions. Its technique for formulating questions can be learned in just a few minutes, and then practiced in real-life situations by anyone. It is used by students, teachers, parents, health care professionals, patients, voters, and anyone else who seeks more information. These techniques can enhance conversations with families.

The skills and strategies developed using these types of techniques are valuable outside the family engagement realm as well. They can support positive conversations in all spheres where families communicate together. More information about all of these strategies can be found on the websites of the organizations mentioned above.

Safety

Creating spaces for engagement requires openness and honesty from all partners. It also asks for a level of vulnerability from all partners that may not always be comfortable for participants.

When asked to share the most surprising thing she had learned from working with families, one parent educator said she was, "surprised at how well some of our families had hidden some pretty big challenges until they felt able to share. We try to be warm and supportive to all."

– Parents as Teachers National Center [PATNC], *2018 family engagement survey*

To promote open and honest communication, let's think for a minute about the safety of the space. Of course, there is the actual physical safety of the space to consider for any type of engagement event. These physical aspects are the things

Things to consider when trying to establish emotional safety:

- How is your room laid out? When having personal conversations you might want to think about whether you are sitting in rows or in circles. If circles, do you want one circle, or multiple smaller ones? There are many good resources available to support your thinking around room layout.

- Who's sitting next to whom? While you probably won't make people get up and move, do pay attention to body language, and see if it might be beneficial to do an activity that mixes up the seating pattern.

- Who is in the room? Some families may not feel safe sharing their concerns about their child's teacher with the teacher or administrator present. Consider who is invited to participate in group conversations when you are hoping to gather honest data and feedback from families.

we most often think about when planning groups—where the session will be located, how our families will get there, and at what time the event or meeting should occur. Each of these factors impacts how safe families feel, and by identifying and addressing these concerns, you are able to demonstrate to the family that they can trust you.

Whether you hold your events in your own building or out in the community, there are several factors to take into consideration when planning your event. You'll want to be intentional about the time of day, and how parents will arrive. If it will be dark out during or after your meeting, will that affect the safety of the surrounding areas, or of public transportation? If you are going out into the community, consider the same things—how will people get there? Is the neighborhood one where all families will be safe, or are there social dynamics that need to be considered before choosing a place to gather?

While physical safety is important for getting people to attend events, once they arrive families also want to know that there is an emotionally safe space for them to be honest and vulnerable. You might be thinking, *but the topic of this workshop is very simple, so maybe I don't have to think about the environment that much.* But think about it this way: How many times have you been having a simple conversation with someone, just about your everyday life, when a particular topic comes up and the conversation takes an unexpected turn into deeper, more serious territory? You never know when the opportunity might arise for you or your families to dive into deeper conversation that exposes them, or you, in a way that you hadn't anticipated.

While you can't anticipate the direction of every conversation that might happen at an event or group, you can establish some consistent practices that will create a sense of safety for families while they are present. Setting a pattern of expected behaviors, as group agreements or norms, allows families to anticipate a level of confidentiality and respect, no matter the topic of discussion. Facilitators might also think about beginning each gathering with a friendly, low-risk activity or conversation starter that initiates conversations and helps participants to become more mentally present. These types of activities and supports not only allow people that might be meeting for the first time to get to know each other, but also have the potential to interrupt previous negative interactions, and start a new foundation for positive interactions.

Remember, what you do changes the way that others do things! If you communicate and follow through with families, you can lead and support other staff in building their own capacity to be accountable.

Accountability

Another way organizations support trust is by making sure that everyone is doing what they said they would do. The smallest detail, easily overlooked or brushed to the side, may be the one thing that a family is really paying attention to. While following up on our commitments may seem like a commonsense thing to do, we often find that we, as professionals, fail to follow through. We'll dig into this more in the following chapter.

For the sake of building trust, it truly matters that you make that phone call to check-in when you said you would, even when you don't want to. When you tell parents that you will have something ready for them, have it. Each time that you fulfill your promises to them, you are gaining a little more trust than you had before. That is the kind of trust that builds relationships, and relationships are what encourage engagement.

There is power in being a trendsetter! You have the power to positively influence your organization by setting a trend of trust-building activities and behaviors. As a culture of trust begins to grow, it shapes how others act within that space; this builds webs of trust that spread to all of the relationships around you. Building trust is cyclical; when someone trusts another person, they are more likely to act in ways that encourage others to trust in them as well. For example, when we, as staff, demonstrate to families that we will follow through on what we said we would do, families are, in turn, more likely to follow through on what they said they would do, too.

Consistency

Being consistent, which goes hand in hand with being accountable, is another simple but effective strategy for building trust.

Giving families consistent feedback and messaging may seem like a small thing, but a lack of consistency can create confusion, and does not inspire trust. If your organization has community input meetings that are always changing time and location, without consistent communication, it can be hard for people to know when and where to show up. Families may feel like you are intentionally making it difficult to attend, and that you do not actually want their feedback, regardless of your intention. Trying to make gatherings more accessible by alternating locations may show thoughtfulness on your part, but these types of strategies can backfire if communication isn't consistent and accessible. As predictability increases a feeling of trust, it also contributes to an overall sense of emotional stability.

reflection

Which strategies for encouraging honest dialogue with families might be the best fit for your organization?

In what ways is your organization or school already ensuring the physical and emotional safety of families during engagement activities?

What practices do you have in place that can support staff and administrators in being accountable and consistent?

Consider investing in staff and family development about psychological safety and open communication. This can go a long way to develop trusting relationships.

Deepening trust

Trust is complex—especially in the context of engaging families. There are many ways to build trust, and many of the examples that we have talked about so far have been focused on laying a foundation of trust, and creating the conditions in which trust can take root. Perhaps your organization is already experiencing the benefits of a growing trust with families, seeing positive outcomes in children, and looking to continue on this path. How can we take the level of trust we've been building even further, as an entire organization?

Decision making

As families begin to engage with your organization or school, they may seek out opportunities to engage at various levels and places. Think about where your organization currently engages families. Do parents volunteer to do tasks, assist in the classroom, or lead groups? How often does your organization let families in on important decisions?

Providing families with input on decisions builds trust both ways. As families make decisions that improve the organization, families' knowledge and expertise become more apparent to staff. This opens doors for additional opportunities for input.

Families will begin to see organizations differently as they see staff and administrators actively seeking out their opinions, and then see those opinions or decisions put into practice. Highlighting the value in their expertise, through implementation, can go a long way in creating a trusting relationship. Ask your families for observations and suggestions and take that feedback into account when making decisions.

Also, it's important to consider where, and how, families are already asking your institution to engage with them. These may not be direct asks, but think about where families often have the most questions, suggestions, or feedback. Being able to recognize areas where families have interest, and building opportunities for engagement in those areas demonstrates to families that the organization is listening to them. When families feel as though they are being heard, they will continue to engage in the processes as they become available. Feeling truly heard is a key component in building and deepening trust.

Take, for example, a parent who, during a home visit, repeatedly asks the parent educator questions about early literacy, and expresses a desire to learn more about early literacy and connect with other parents around this topic. The parent educator in this scenario may be able to partner with the parent to facilitate a group connection with other parents interested in this topic. This type of attention demonstrates real listening by the professional, and helps to forge trust.

There is much more to hearing families than simply listening to their words. Including their input in decisions, and being willing to negotiate when feasible, demonstrates that organizations are integrating families' feedback. When it comes to building trust, engaging families in decision-making processes says to them that the organization not only values but also trusts their input, which continues the cycle of building trust.

Staff capacity

Many schools and organizations are consciously trying to create spaces for families to engage. At the same time that organizations are looking deeply at how they are improving family involvement, they also need to turn that gaze inward, and look honestly at their own organization in order to determine where, and how, they are actually willing to engage families. This is where we challenge your organization

It can feel intimidating, or uncertain at times, when families are more actively involved in the decision-making process. Organizations may fear that they are letting go of too much power and control. Explore how shared decision making can strengthen your organization and, ultimately, how it can impact your outcomes.

to think more deeply about what it truly means to engage families. In some places, that might look like creating family nights and presenting material for learning and growing together. In other places it might look like having parent representatives on the board. It looks like both of these, plus so much more! Nevertheless, these plans and intentions for engagement might not give you the results you hope for—unless you are giving a solid look at evaluating your organization as a whole. An essential part of family engagement in your organization must be your staff's capacity and willingness to engage families in the ways you have outlined. Making it clear how you intend for families to engage without follow through from the whole organization or the whole school will only damage the work that has been done to build trust within all parties.

For families to truly be engaged, there must be equal buy-in from staff members at all levels. Families can do their best to get involved, but until the members of the organization accept families' input, engagement is simply one sided. Take into consideration that staff may also need support or professional development and coaching to strengthen their knowledge and their skills around engaging families. If levels of trust are not yet high, and the organization is asking staff to provide these opportunities for parents, it may be especially important to highlight the mutual benefits of trust and engagement. Support staff with research that shows them that when families and schools trust each other, and work together, children and schools have better outcomes. Many professionals entered their field with interest and aptitude in supporting children. A somewhat different set of skills is needed to engage their families.

An essential aspect of genuine involvement in trust-building is to provide staff with opportunities for on-going conversations and reflections. Staff need the chance to brainstorm authentic ways for them implement these strategies, both individually and collectively, and time to share challenges. Don't forget to ask staff for their input, ideas, and strategies for engaging families! In what ways do they already involve families in decision-making, track their own accountability, and create safe physical and emotional spaces? What are some new ideas they might want to try that seem like a good fit, for both themselves and their families?

Community integration

Inviting families into your organization's space is an important part of engagement, but how often do you go into theirs? Are you showing up at community events or intentionally organizing events across the community, in spaces where your families live and work? Extending the scope of school events to encompass the whole community can speak volumes to your families. We don't always think about

Things to think about

■ Be consistent

■ Negotiate

■ Create safe places

how often we ask families to come into our space, our comfort zones, without ever stepping into theirs. Build trust by saying: I'm willing to go out of my comfort zone and into your space as well. I'm willing to let you (the families) be the experts in the space that also greatly impacts your child.

One parent educator, new in her position, was surprised by the fact that, "families *want* us in their homes. It was not something I was used to in previous jobs, and to be welcomed into someone's home feels like such an honor and a privilege." By entering families' space in engagement activities, you are opening up entirely new possibilities for trust to grow. When a family invites you into a personal or community space, there is a lot of potential for relationships to flourish and deepen in trust.

Inter-organizational work

Building and maintaining trust within your organization is a big part of building a healthy environment for staff and administrators. How you reach out to build trust in the community that your organization serves is another vital, and sometimes more challenging, task. The ways you work with other organizations that serve families impacts how those families will see you, and in turn if, and how, they will trust you. If your organization has taken the time to create meaningful community connections that support the growth and development of families and their children, you may see families who are more engaged with you. Families understand that not all of their needs can be met by one organization, but they will appreciate that your organization recognizes their additional needs, as well as your attempts to understand the other organizations that they are engaged with. Through collaboration, organizations have the capacity to teach each other a lot about how to best partner with families in the community.

A unique example of inter-organizational collaboration and community engagement is the partnership that's been created between Normandy Schools Collaborative and Wyman Center—a non-profit in the greater St. Louis area. The partnership was created to address the multi-faceted needs of students that could not be addressed by schools, yet were impacting the lives of the children within the district. Over 35 non-profits have come together, "to share experiences and information, to create better alignment of services so that youth have what they need, when they need it." By collaborating with other organizations that provide services that fall outside the realm of the school's expertise, they're demonstrating that they can be trusted to support the whole child. By investing in this kind of partnership, the district is rebuilding trust in schools that had previously been weakened or broken.

When organizations acknowledge that one program alone cannot support all of the needs of families, they are more likely to cooperate. Families are more likely to stay engaged if they see that they can get various needs met through organizations that communicate well with each other.

reflection

What are some ways to integrate families into decision making?

How often do you enter spaces where families work and live?

What opportunities can you provide staff for authentic reflection and application of trust-building strategies?

Trust

Trust forms the basis of solid relationships. Once trust is established, we can really go after our vision and goals together—and handle the inevitable challenges along the way.

moving forward

There are many aspects to trust. Take a moment to reflect on the previous chapter and think about which ideas, strategies, or pieces of trust are strongest, and which require growth.

- > **Trust through transitions**
- > **Trust and respect**
- > **Distrust**
- > **Moving forward**
- > **Honest conversations**
- > **Safety**
- > **Accountability**
- > **Consistency**
- > **Decision making**
- > **Staff capacity**
- > **Community integration**
- > **Inter-organizational work**

We're strong on this:

We're so-so at this:

We're working on it:

Respect

R-E-S-P-E-C-T. It's an emotionally-charged word, with many different meanings to many different people. Long before it was made famous by Aretha Franklin, respect was cited as the magic ingredient in many strong relationships—and the missing link in many fragile ones. We started this book discussing the importance of trust, but trust cannot be built without a foundation of mutual respect, and successful engagement of families depends on it.

So, what does respect mean to us and the families we want to engage? What does respect translated into action really look like?

Despite the fact that people frequently refer to the importance and necessity of respect, there is often confusion about exactly what "respecting others" means. Part of this is personal; we each determine as individuals what it means to respect, and to be respected. There are also a lot of factors related to respect that can be culturally specific. Most often, our personal understanding of what respect is, and how it feels, is based on our culture—where we come from, our family values, and many other influences.

Take the initiative

The Ontario Capacity Building Series, citing Micheal Fullan, notes we may need to demonstrate "respect for others before [we] have earned the right to be respected... and then do the things that build... trust over time." As the saying goes: we have to give it to get it. Building relationships based on mutual respect can feel like an uphill battle at first. Keep in mind, if you are hoping to receive respect, you may need to offer it first.

Foundations of respect

Even though we may find respect difficult to pin down, each of us is aware when we are the recipients of a particular kind of positive attention; we can feel respect, especially when we sense that someone holds us in high regard. This feeling is transmittable across cultures and transcends personal variations of what respect looks and feels like. A person doesn't need to be an expert in cross-cultural communication to be able to transmit a feeling of respect across cultural or linguistic lines. While respect is complex, and understanding differs from person to person, there are some universal components we can tap into and focus on.

Non-judgement

Respect can also sometimes be mistakenly equated with "liking" or approval, but you can still respect someone as a person, even if you do not like something they do. For example, a professional may not "like" or approve of how a family is behaving in some particular way, based on their own views of parenting. Just because they don't agree with the actions, however, does not mean that they don't respect that family and the way they care for their child— as long as no harm is occurring. Likewise, parents may not like the approach that their child's teacher has taken, but if they feel confident that the teacher cares for and is safely doing what they believe is best to support their child, they can still respect the teacher's decisions.

Where difference of opinion has the potential to cross into the realm of disrespect is when judgement enters the picture. Our own views, likes and dislikes, and family influences shape how we perceive the actions of others. At times, school and organizational staff may have a negative view or personal bias about the way a family is raising a child; this disapproval is often very apparent to families, even if attempts are made to disguise it. Not surprisingly, if and when someone feels like they are being judged negatively, they are likely to interpret that feeling as disrespect. If families feel disrespected in their parenting practices, or staff in their educating practices, it can be very difficult to connect around anything, even topics regarding the child. Feelings of judgement that are experienced as disrespect often create walls that are challenging to overcome in building good relationships.

Whether or not you are in full agreement with all the families and staff that make up your organization, establishing mutual respect is critical to building relationships with all of your partners in family engagement. Mutual respect can, and often does, exist in relationships despite there being differences in opinion, or preferences about the way things "should" be done.

Collaboration

Authors in *Stress and Quality of Working Life: Interpersonal and Occupation- Based Stress* note that appreciation, acceptance, and respect from the individuals we deem as important in our lives are so meaningful that they have been categorized as basic human needs. We communicate our appreciation, acceptance

Respecting the work families are doing

It is important to remember that parents are children's first and most influential teachers. Take a moment to appreciate everything that parents have done to get their child to this point in life. Before entering school, their child is walking, talking, and meeting other developmental milestones that require social interaction to develop. Parents continually show up at the door to let you into their home for home visits, despite all of the other events and priorities in their busy lives. They help with homework. They feed and clothe their child. Every family is doing the best they can with what they have. These are not minor accomplishments, and they are worthy of respect as they move their children towards healthy, successful futures. When you find yourself feeling challenged by the work that you are doing, or struggling to find respect, it can be helpful to reflect on all of the incredible strengths that parents have.

and respect all the time in our daily interactions with others—via verbal feedback, fair treatment, and even body language. As adults, we may not often reflect on how this communication has developed over time, but it's worth revisiting the process. Although it is not likely that we have the clearest of memories of grade school, this is the time many of us received our first formal training in the foundations of respect. We were taught to be tolerant, share, and above all, work together. Listed below are the grade-level outcomes for Physical Education from the Society of Health and Physical Educators; they come from the educational standard that evaluates how students exhibit respect for self and others:

- Starting in kindergarten, children are learning the basics of sharing equipment and space with others.

- In first grade, they work independently with others in a variety of environments (such as small and large groups).

- Second grade brings an expectation that students will work independently with others as partners.

- For third grade, they work cooperatively with others and—importantly—praise others for their success

- In fourth grade, a new distinction emerges. Students praise the performance of others, both more and less skilled than themselves, and accept players of all skill levels into the physical activity.

- Finally, by the end of fifth grade, they accept, recognize, and actively involve others with both higher and lower abilities into physical activities and group projects.

It's nice to imagine that we all mastered the "working with others" standard back in elementary school—and that we're still using those skills now.

Collaborative conversations

Collaborative conversations can deliver effective solutions that are more sustainable than those decided by the organization alone. For example, when trying to resolve a behavior issue a child is having, the conversation might sound something like this: "Here's what I've noticed works in this space. What do you do that works well at home, that we can bring here and try, too? How do we make these two places more similar for your child in order to support his or her success?" Prompts like these engage families in partnership around their children's behavior supports, and contribute to relationships that are based on trust and mutual respect. These relationships encourage families to continue to engage as they feel validated and heard as part of a team—and to explore new ways of doing so. Making conversations reciprocal—a partnership—instead of a one-way information stream from the school out to families, can greatly impact children's outcomes for the better as reactions and supports become consistent between school and home.

While we learned the value of working together when we were children, the training that we have had as adults, particularly in certain professions, has led us to lean on skills that look a lot more like giving information, directing, or informing others, rather than working collaboratively. Despite our true motivations, we can be unintentionally condescending to families, or even come across as bossy or invasive, when we simply tell them what to do. While giving instructions or information may come naturally to you and doesn't feel like "telling", it may not always be the best approach. You may be missing out on valuable information that can support you if you're not spending time listening to and planning with families.

By listening, educators and professionals can support families in building upon what they have, and integrating what families do well into practices at the organization. Working together and building on families' strengths demonstrates a respect for what families are bringing to the table, and avoids indicating that your way is better than theirs.

The State Advisory Council for Parent Involvement in Education points out "the more parents perceive teachers as valuing their contributions, keeping them informed, and providing them with suggestions, the higher parental engagement in their children's learning." In other words, the more we talk to families in a way that lets them know we are listening and working towards the same goals, the more families will talk with us. This can be done in a variety of ways—letters home, emails, or conversations at pickup or drop off all offer opportunities to touch base with families about the goals that have been set, and what is being done to reach them.

Respect is an essential component of establishing good relationships with families. The best ways to approach forming this foundation of mutual respect is by opening the lines of communication, and demonstrating to families that the organization is truly listening and applying what it learns. This means communicating the message: "We want to learn about you and your family. Once you share information with us, we are going to demonstrate to you that the information you have shared is valuable."

Think about a time when you disagreed with a family over a parenting practice. How were you able to take a step back and still support the family with their choice?

In what ways are you collaborating with families to make decisions about supports for children?

Gathering information

Learning more about the families you'll be partnering with is an essential first step in creating a relationship based on mutual respect. In order to gather relevant information from families, you may use both formal and informal information channels. Each type of information gathering has benefits and challenges, and depending on the type of information you are looking to gather, you may choose one or a combination of strategies.

Surveys

Your organization or school may wish to develop and utilize a family information survey that will allow you to quickly gather some standard information from families. Because surveys are a formal tool, they can come across as "gathering data" and feel impersonal—unless care is taken to make them more personal and less like paperwork. Think about how you might personalize a survey by asking about things such as what the family does for fun, how their child learns best, or what their favorite foods are. Questions like these, when mixed in with more standard measurement questions, can contribute to you getting to know the family better and make the survey feel less like a form. Think also about how you can explain to families why you are gathering the information. When people understand the reasoning behind why they are doing something, they are more likely to engage and be honest.

from the field

One parent highlighted how her school used family bios to gather information about each child and family at the beginning of the year. They asked questions about who lives in the home, when and how is the best time to communicate, what parents' jobs are, and other questions that were not overly personal but allowed the school to get to know them better. This strategy gave staff the opportunity to learn things like whether a family was a single-parent family, what parents' work schedules were, or if a family had any fun traditions that they might want to share. It created more opportunities for successful interactions and communication by asking when and how was the best way to communicate with each parent. This parent recounted how it also was clear to her that the school was using this information. They didn't just gather the information, but read it and applied it. It meant a lot to her to know that they actually respected her time, and her family's situation, and she didn't have to continually remind them about aspects of her personal life that were impacting her child.

One-on-one conversations

While surveys are a good tool to get a lot of information quickly, we challenge you to think more deeply about how you connect through the survey. Perhaps you use surveys as an entry point into person-to-person conversations, or maybe they are a template that you use to guide follow-up conversations with families. Experts at the Search Institute confirm that face-to-face conversations will build and deepen relationships with families in a way that a survey or questionnaire simply cannot. You may also find families who are willing to engage in a conversation who will not fill out a paper survey.

Things to consider

When gathering information from families, either by survey or in one-on-one conversations, it may be beneficial to take time to consider the following:

- **Language on the survey.** Pay attention to the reading level and readability of the survey (if it is written). You do not want to confuse families, especially if this is the first point of contact that you have with them. Also consider the home language of family. Is it possible to create the survey or conduct a conversation in their home language? This extra effort will not only demonstrate your respect for families' home culture, but will also allow you to gather more information.

- **Who is gathering the information.** The person who has the conversation with families might impact the knowledge that you will gain from them. Make sure that whoever has the conversation or administers the survey, it is a logical person to be interacting with the family. It might be a teacher or administrator—preferably someone who will be interacting with the family on a regular basis. This ensures that those emotional cues are understood by those who need them most, and provides a sense of security for the family that their information stays with only those who need it.

- **Who gives information.** While it can be tempting to just talk with mom, because she is easier to reach, you will get a much better picture of the child and his or her family if you can talk to all primary caregivers of the child—whether that is mom and dad, or dad and grandma. You also will want to think about capturing the information in multiple households if the child lives in multiple places. Gathering family information from each part of the family will demonstrate your respect for the influence of each person who cares for the child.

- **When information gathering takes place.** It is most helpful to gather information when the child first interacts with you and your organization, but this is not the only time. Informal conversations over time can help you keep up-to-date, and you may wish to do formal data collection annually or every six months. Be careful to not ask too frequently as to overwhelm parents and reduce their participation.

A survey can provide you with what you have specifically asked for, but a conversation may lead to additional information that you might not have even thought to ask about—information that might impact the child profoundly. For example, when asking about who lives in the home, the reply you might get on a survey would read, "mom, siblings, grandma". In a conversation, however, you might learn that this family has migrated from another country where the child's father is still living, and that the child maintains a strong relationship with his dad through phone connections. Without a conversation, you might assume this family is a single-parent home, or that the child's father is not actively involved in the child's life. You might also learn about how having a long-distance relationship impacts the child, and what you can do to comfort him if he gets sad or overwhelmed.

In addition, you will gather emotional information and understand how a family feels about the answers to their questions through tone and body language during a one-on-one conversation. You might see a mom's eyes light up when she talks about her favorite family activity, or hear dad get frustrated when he tells you about challenges they have had at school in the past. These emotions are a part of getting to know a family more deeply, and are difficult to convey in writing.

Helping families find their strengths

You may have to be creative in seeking out ways for families to support their children and the work they are doing. Not everyone will be aware of how their skill set fits within the larger organization. Staff may need to listen closely to how they can integrate families as partners in processes.

For example, you might overhear a parent talking about how much they love cooking their favorite meal and ask them if they would like to lead a parent group around making the recipe, or if they could contribute a meal they've cooked with their child for an upcoming event, if you provide the supplies. Cooking might not be a strength that they even knew had a place in your organization!

Surveys and conversations are tools to gather data, not only about children, but also about what strengths the family can bring to your organization and where they might best engage. Once data is gathered, it is up to you to follow through on using that data to strengthen the programming and support for the child. This reinforces the message to families that they are partners in the organizations providing support to their child, not just someone who uses the services that you provide.

reflection

What are some ways that you can get to know the skills and knowledge of your families?

How could you integrate families' knowledge into existing programs and activities?

Respect for home and its impact

Understanding what is going on at home, and the ways that it impacts families and children, exhibits that you respect families' wider systems. Families don't exist in isolation; they are influenced by forces within the family itself, as well as from outside agencies and individuals. The pressures and challenges of time, work, finances, and other obligations all compete for the time and energy of families. When you use surveys or have conversations for gathering data, you might gain some of this knowledge; other information about home life you will gather along the way, as it becomes relevant to whatever is happening in the child's development and education. Some pieces of a child's home life you might not ever learn about, but they will still impact how the child moves through his or her day and handles emotions and learning. Acknowledging that there may be a lot going on is the first step; how you process and apply the information you have about families' home lives is the next.

Listening and remembering

You took the time to gather information about families, and now it is time to make sure that the information is reflected appropriately in your processes and interactions with the family. Remembering which kids are being raised by grandma and grandpa, and being sure to call families at a time that they indicated worked for them, are two examples of how you can easily show families you have listened. While it might seem like a small gesture, it can go a long way in reducing stress for families and reducing friction in the relationship. It may seem like a minor transgression if you forget or slip up, but repeated actions that don't acknowledge what the family has told you can create cracks in relationships that are difficult to mend. It's not hard to imagine why a person might feel disrespected or dismissed if she is asked about the best time or way to contact her, and that information is ignored or forgotten repeatedly.

Rights and boundaries

Working with families, both in schools and in organizations in the community, creates many opportunities for interactions that may blur lines of professional and personal relationships. You may have a professional code of ethics to guide your actions, but each organization should also have policies and guidelines to ensure that common boundaries are set. A few things to consider as you either review or develop your organizations policies and practices are:

- Be knowledgeable on the rights of families in your organization or field. There are some laws that clearly determine rights, such as the Every Student Succeeds Act, or the Individuals with Disabilities in Education Act, but be sure to consider other legal or organizational rules as well.

- Know who to talk to when you get into a situation that tests boundaries or brings up an ethical dilemma. Often there is not a clear right course of action, and it can be helpful to discuss possible scenarios with a supervisor or colleague.

- Be aware of the policies and practices within your organization around things like going into homes, accepting meals, connections on social media, and other potential issues. Knowing what boundaries exist in advance can help reduce potential conflicts.

Respecting privacy

Remember that information families share with you should not be public knowledge. They are trusting you with personal history that does not need to be a topic of conversation with other staff. Use discretion in sharing information based on who might benefit from knowing, and always have a conversation with the family about what you will share, with whom, and why, before you share any knowledge. If you are able to ask families for permission before sharing, do so. Each of these gestures lets families know that you value them and respect that their family information is theirs to control.

Solutions to stressors

If it is within your ability, it can be beneficial to support the family in finding potential solutions to stressors that the family has shared with you. We cannot and should not try to "fix" everything. But what we can do is work within our realm and partner with families to manage the impact of outside stressors on children within our walls.

Schools and organizations address these stressors in multiple ways. Some are able to provide bus passes or transportation vouchers so that families can attend events and conferences if transportation is a challenge. Several schools are now working to integrate washing machines into their buildings so that children and families are able to wash clothing for free or a minimal fee, increasing confidence and attendance rates. Other organizations offer children a place to sleep or have snacks at the front desk for those who are not getting enough sleep or food at home for any number of reasons. Children may need additional time to work on homework that cannot be done at home, or individualized attention if they have working parents who are unable to support the completion of work. Providing opportunities like these for all children acknowledges that there is more to their lives than what happens at school, and that sometimes families need reinforcements to get basic needs met.

For many families, it is a good thing that organizations are aware of their stressors and are actively thinking of ways to reduce the impact of those stressors on their children. Remember that every family defines their own stressors differently, and that what may seem to be a stressor for one family might not be for another family. How we approach families regarding stressors is also incredibly important. Not everyone wants stressors to be known, and some families will not appreciate what you might feel is helpful. Explore what resources the family already has, both within and through external supports, before offering your own recommendations or resources. Having a discussion about why you might be offering support, or have a concern, before offering suggestions will set up a context where families will be much more likely to partner with you to address the impacts of these stressors on children.

from the field

One parent recalled that, when her children were infants, they were at a daycare center where she felt very respected; the center honored her choices at home, and was trying to integrate them into the children's time at the daycare. One time period that stuck out in her memory was when she was breastfeeding. The center would allow her to come into the class during the day and feed her child whenever she was able (she worked close to the center). She reflected on how important this flexibility was and how she felt embraced by the staff, who did not mind when she came at different times—even if it wasn't during the time they had set in the schedule for parent visitation. She also recognized that it created more work for them, not only to use breastmilk when her baby was drinking from a bottle, but also to let her be a part of the day on her schedule. This welcome of her parenting practices and willingness to be flexible built a strong relationship with the staff and kept her coming back.

Vetting resources

For those families that may need additional support, or have stressors that are outside your organizational capacity, it is beneficial to have referrals to outside resources available. Make sure to vet resources to ensure they are valid and current, and avoid accidentally providing false information. Making personal connections with a few local, frequently used resources can help you to stay current about what is available, and let families know you aren't just providing generic resources that you don't actually know anything about.

reflection

In what ways does your organization or school currently address family stressors?

What might you be able to do that you are not currently doing—while working within your budget and policies?

Respecting identities

Respect is a multi-faceted component of interacting with and engaging families. It can be demonstrated by finding out and building on families' knowledge and skills, but it also includes respecting *who* they are. As we all know, each family has its own look and feel—just think about your own family members and what makes them who they are if you need an example!

Like each school, each family creates and operates on its own set of invisible rules and principles, some of which may be familiar to you, and some of which may look very different from the rules and principles that exist in your own family. We know that identities are complex, and each individual defines his or her own identity in extremely personal ways. Though more overt indicators of identity, like class, race, or ethnicity can be important to a person's sense of identity, there are so many other aspects that contribute to each person and families' sense of who they are: values, thoughts, political beliefs, personal histories, and so on. In the context of family engagement, this means avoiding stereotypes and making room for unique individual and family identities.

The unique culture inside of each individual home might include what role each parent has, or what rules there are around homework or playtime. When you know how a family operates, you can get a better sense of who is involved, and how that translates to their involvement with your organization. There is traditionally less engagement with fathers in children's education, but many times we just haven't asked in the right way to bring fathers in. How do you tie their roles at home into the roles at the school to demonstrate that you understand, and are alright with

from the field

When families are respected they can feel it, just as you can. Body language and communication say a lot about the power dynamics and respect that exist between people. The language we use—both the words and the tone—is a way that respect is communicated clearly between individuals. Just as in any other circumstances, words matter! How families are referred to, and even the names of the programs themselves, can send a message. New York Times author Sandra Larson notes that First Teacher, a grassroots parenting empowerment program in Massachusetts, is very mindful of the language they select to talk about their work.

"Language matters when ensuring that parents don't feel judged. Ms. Shepherd, a parent herself, uses terms like 'our kids" and 'we' instead of 'they' or 'clients'. It [First Teacher] aims not to 'serve the disadvantaged' but to 'build social capital', by which they mean the kind of empowering web of resources and social and professional connections that white middle-class parents may take for granted."

how they choose to engage? You can then leverage the relationships to shift engagement patterns if you feel it would be beneficial.

Asking questions to learn about family culture is just one way to demonstrate respect. You might also consider observing religious holidays in your classroom that stray from the standard ones on the school calendar. Some families might be willing to share their experiences with all the families and children in your organization, but others might feel most respected when they are simply allowed to practice as they wish, with no repercussions for missing events or days of school.

When staff begin to address issues or point out strengths *within the context of the families' culture*, they are demonstrating that, not only are they trying to understand the family, they also value what they are doing within their home.

Consider culture: communication, sensitivity, and respect

"I think that we have to remember that even people who are impoverished, oppressed, who have a splayed legacy, historical trauma—that they have knowledge to bring to the table as well. So then when you start looking at that, we have to figure out what that language is between us and them, ... [so] that we can all get on the same page in terms of language and how we view culture."

– Renea Butler-King, social worker

While we will dive deeper into culture and diversity in the chapter "Integration", we want to make sure to mention it here as well. Not only is respect for cultural diversity a large part of respect overall, but each of our cultures shapes how we define respect as well. Cultural competence includes respect for a variety of communication styles, and awareness of the cultural influences and preferences of those with whom we partner.

What families bring to the conversation and to the table is invaluable knowledge, and it is important that we know and learn to communicate effectively with families.

Finding shared communicative ground is a challenge that often exists when two or more communication styles come into play in any given scenario. As with any other aspect of identity, there are cultural as well as personal influences on our communication style. Sociolinguist Deborah Tanner studied communication and communication styles as perceived across gender, cultural, and ethnic lines, in her book, *You Just Don't Understand*. Her findings reflect how often our own backgrounds influence our expectations around communication norms, and the ways in which we judge other styles negatively that are different than our own.

Despite these influences, one does not need to be an expert in communication styles in order to communicate respectfully with all families. Not all parents will

from the field

Parent educators who are conducting home visits are given a first-hand look into families' cultures. While it can be incredibly beneficial, these visits also can provide plenty of opportunities for misunderstandings or collisions of cultures. One parent shared the story of the first time the parent educator from her Parents as Teachers program came to her home. This visit happened many years ago, but still sticks out in her mind as a clear demonstration of the respect this person had for her home. When the parent educator walked in the door, the first thing she asked was whether the parent preferred that she keep her shoes on or off. While this might seem like a simple gesture, it showed that she was concerned about following this parent's home practices, setting the tone for further interactions that were to happen within the home.

Allowing someone into your home is an incredibly vulnerable position to be in for some families. Asking them what they do when they are home, or what they prefer that you do when you are in their home, demonstrates a level of respect for their home rules, just like you would anticipate them to follow the rules when they enter your building.

express concern, describe behavior, or talk about their child's actions and progress in the same way. Along with a unique identity, each family has its own way of communicating; in order to truly understand each other, we have to be willing to meet families half way—always keeping in mind and respecting the family's insight and the value of what they are contributing to the conversation. In this way, listening is also a fundamental aspect of respect.

reflection

In what ways does your organization represent families' individual identities in the work that you do?

How have you experienced cultural influences on communication with the families in your community?

Allowing for a deeper level of partnership

"It is the goal of the Departments that all early childhood systems recognize and support families as essential partners in providing services that improve children's development, learning, and wellness."

– U.S. Departments of Education and Health and Human Services, *Policy Statement on Family Engagement*

For many organizations, realizing the vision of a true and equal partnership with families means that some changes need to occur. Though we believe in this vision, and want to work toward achieving it, we know it is challenging.

Sometimes, current structural supports in institutions do not support this ideal, and changes may need to occur in policies, practices, language, and attitudes toward partnership. We know that if we truly want to demonstrate respect, it is most effective when it comes from every staff member and individual.

Ultimately, families will know when they, and their ideas, are respected. This is when they begin to see themselves as partners in the processes of your organization.

Understanding partnership as an organization

It may be helpful for your staff to have a conversation about what "partnering with families" means to each of them. When everyone is on the same page, and there is a general understanding of what partnering means, families are more likely to feel comfortable engaging. Consistency in conversations and implementation of engagement efforts by all staff (and in turn, respect towards families by all staff) are key to success. When each person that a family interacts with demonstrates the same approach and respect for the family's knowledge, parents will want to continue to engage.

To prepare to have these conversations, support your staff and leaders in understanding the enormous impacts on outcomes that occur when families are engaged in as many parts of their child's development and education as possible. Invite them to grow together as you recognize the inevitable bumps and bruising along the way, in order to get to a point where partnership is happening. Acknowledge upfront that partnership does not mean things will always be smooth. Collaboration takes time, and can lead to uncomfortable conversations and interactions that test both staff and families alike. There are always challenges to maintaining balance. Nevertheless, we believe, and research supports, that weathering those bumps and finding balance with families ultimately creates successful partnerships and positive outcomes.

"The NCPFCE [National Center on Parent, Family, and Community Engagement] also recommends that family engagement efforts be **Systemic** and **Comprehensive**. Think of family engagement as being baked INTO the cake, not just as icing on the top of the cake that looks nice. It is best when family engagement is integrated throughout all aspects of programming."

– **Kim Engelman**, *Family Engagement: What IS IT and what does it LOOK LIKE?*

Process for collaborative goal setting

There are many examples of how an organization might demonstrate respect for families through partnership and collaboration. This includes opening up processes that are often done internally to include families' input. One example is the way in which your organization sets goals, both for individual children and families, as well as for the organization as a whole. Goals that are set in collaboration with families allow all voices and views to be heard and considered when the final goals are identified. It does take effort to ensure that families are not only a part of the goal design, but that their input is reflected in the goals themselves. Also, consider how families will contribute to reaching those goals and how their voices are reflected in the action steps identified.

Reflect on the process below for creating a more collaborative goal-setting process:

1. Identify stakeholders (including families, your staff, children if applicable, other community agencies or supports).

2. Form a committee of those individuals, and ask stakeholders who is missing from the table; invite them in if appropriate. You may have different ideas of who are stakeholders than others. Listen to their ideas about why they believe that person or agency is a stakeholder before eliminating anyone from consideration.

3. Create goals for organization and individuals that utilize the whole community in the process, and give people an opportunity to be engaged and have their ideas reflected in final goals.

Be honest about why your organization is not engaging families in certain places—is it because it would be a challenge to do so and maintain best practices? Or is it because it is challenging or uncomfortable personally? If you truly want to engage families at all levels, your organization will need to have some honest conversations about what that might look like, and how comfortable everyone is with letting families have influence in places where they typically might not have before.

Staff may express concerns throughout the course of these conversations. These may include valid questions about whether or not it is efficient or helpful to be fully driven by family input at the deepest levels (for example, in budgeting or personnel decisions). However, even in those places, there are opportunities to partner with families to gain insight and influence the processes.

Deeper partnership often means we become willing to do things differently. As mentioned in the previous chapter "Trust", you may want to consider professional

Family influence on data collection

Conversations with parents about data collection can lead you to awareness about a previously unknown yet important factor that might be influencing a certain data point. For example, one mother shared about a time when her child was taking part in a developmental screening. During this screening the child did not feed herself, which was interpreted as a delay. The parent shared that the child could probably feed herself, but in their culture this was not the norm. As the mother, she did all of the feeding, even when the child was developmentally able to do so independently. When she had a conversation with her parent educator about this evaluation, they were able to identify the missing cultural consideration, and have her child demonstrate the same skill in a different manner. Her child was no longer inaccurately marked as having a delay. Without having had this conversation, neither parent nor parent educator may have realized that the data was skewed.

development opportunities, and identify other ways to provide staff with time and tools to examine and reflect on family engagement and partnership.

Information and data

Respecting parents includes gathering knowledge, but it also includes demonstrating that you believe in the family's capacity to understand and embrace the information that you are giving them. This includes letting families in on the rationale, benchmarks, or evaluation methods used in data collection, as well as equipping families with key terminology about data and outcomes.

Data collection is a large part of how organizations grow, and continue to support families. You may collect data about how families function at home, and how that impacts their children's development. You might also collect data as an organization to see how your practices are impacting outcomes. This data may be around early childhood development, grades, learning potential, or behavior, and all of it should be shared with families.

Behind the curtain

In addition to sharing results, engagement experts note that empowering parents with knowledge of the ways that you, or others, have collected and interpreted data about their child demonstrates that you respect their ability to understand and engage with the entire process. Sharing the process, and the rationale behind it, can be powerful! Having conversations and gathering feedback about the data-collection process also gives your organization an opportunity to understand what families are feeling and thinking when it comes to the activities on which you are collecting data. In addition, families can provide cultural considerations and  other factors that might support your data collection. For example, just explaining how something—especially something that seems intangible—is measured can be extremely useful for parents moving forward. This knowledge can lend structure to conversations that parents are having with staff as well.

Continue to keep in mind that engaging families goes beyond imparting data or information. It means that you are sharing the data and working together on improving outcomes, as partners.

Create a common language

Engaging families successfully requires that they operate from a similar baseline of knowledge as the organization. As professionals, you've most likely had to take at least a few classes or training programs that formalized your learning about early childhood development and/or education. Once you arrived at your job, there were probably opportunities for continued learning about early childhood, education, and your organization, in both formal and informal settings. This has given you a specialized language to use when you talk about the work you do.

Demonstrating respect for families means that they are being given the time and tools they need to be a part of this conversation as a partner, and not just talked at. Be aware of the acronyms and terminology you use, and be respectful by creating a shared language with families. For more in-depth examples of this, look to the chapter "Accessibility".

Another way to engage families in learning and information sharing is to create dual-education streams where families and staff are learning at the same time. Arranging and planning for organization-wide educational sessions, which include families, can demonstrate to families that you are not trying to "catch them up" or that you believe they need a separate way of learning information. These learning opportunities support the creation of the same baseline of knowledge and language, and create a sense of partnership as everyone learns side by side. By opening up staff professional development to families, for example, you can take advantage of the opportunity for engagement with staff outside of typically staff-

Types of Data

The following are some examples of data you might share with families about their child:

- Developmental milestones or screening
- Behavior-tracking data such as an ABC chart
- Grades or other academic skills tests

led events. These interactions can lead to a better understanding of each other, and greater levels of respect for what each party does to contribute to positive child outcomes.

Share what you have

Sharing data with families in a way that balances being approachable, yet does not underestimate their capacity for understanding, is an important way to demonstrate respect for them and for their roles in raising their child. Families also can benefit from knowing the data collected about their child, and they might be able to provide insight to explain the data that staff cannot. There are many ways to engage families in this process, both at data collection and information sharing stages.

When sharing information, think about how and what you share. Do not assume that families do or do not need certain information, or that they already know something that you have might have additional data around, such as a behavior chart tracking a known behavior problem. If families find out that you have information about their child that you have not shared, it can feel like a break in trust and can harm the relationship. It may also feel like you do not believe in their capacity to understand the information. On the other hand, having conversations with parents about the data, as well as offering opportunities for families to learn about their child's education, can be a great starting point for building a partnership.

Learning and conversing with staff and other families can also create a variety of opportunities for data and information to come alive. Each parent learns differently and will appreciate being given an option to receive information in the way that best suits his or her learning style. You may offer

Worth noting is the fact that in order to share data, we must first understand it ourselves. Some data tracking or evaluation systems are confusing and convoluted. Take time to reflect on how user-friendly the systems your organization is using are.

opportunities for families to dig into the data themselves by sending home packets of information, or by providing logins to sites where the data is housed. Other families will want to have a one-on-one or group meeting to discuss the data and what it means for their child. Likewise, some families will want the specific details while others would rather not be bogged down by the smaller numbers and prefer to see the big picture.

Offering multiple information access points also demonstrates that your organization respects their time and ability to choose what works best for them, instead of you determining how they should be learning. Offering time for group conversations provides families the time to talk to each other and make sense of the data in multiple ways through teaching and learning with each other.

reflection

Think about sharing data with your families. How does your organization share the data that it collects with families?

Most professionals have access to information from a variety of sources and in a variety of formats. How might you integrate those sources into your communication with parents?

What strategies is your organization using to give families an opportunity to come and learn about what the data you have collected means and how it applies to their child? What additional strategies might you use?

Respect is a value that is difficult to measure and describe. It remains a challenge for so many organizations, including ours, as we continually work to understand what respect is and is not for the families we serve. We know there are so many personal and cultural components that contribute to this feeling of respect, while at the same time respect is universally essential to building strong relationships. We also believe that if we attempt to employ engagement strategies without first demonstrating an authentic  respect for all parties involved, we can't expect to reach the results we aim to achieve. It truly is a two-way street. To demonstrate respect, and grow into deeper partnership with families, all organizations can work on the ways we listen to the information families share with us, and be more intentional about the ways we share information back. Despite the challenges, we know that we'll be building partnerships grounded in respect, which will open doors for open and honest engagement with families.

Respect

Respecting each others' strengths, skills, knowledge, expertise, and experiences helps us start from a position of positive assumptions and empowerment.

moving forward

There are many aspects to respect. Take a moment to reflect on the previous chapter and think about which ideas, strategies, or pieces of respect are strongest, and which require growth.

> **Non-judgement**

> **Collaboration**

> **Surveys**

> **One-on-one conversations**

> **Listening and remembering**

> **Solutions to stressors**

> **Understanding partnership as an organization**

> **Consider culture: communication, sensitivity, and respect**

> **Information and data**

> **Behind the curtain**

> **Create a common language**

> **Share what you have**

We're strong on this:

We're so-so at this:

We're working on it:

Responsibility

The phrase "shared responsibility" is often included in descriptions of family engagement. We hear these words so often that we may not pause to reflect on what they really mean. This chapter gives us an opportunity to think about shared responsibility from a variety of perspectives. We believe that family engagement is everyone's job, but each of our roles in reaching the end goal look a little different.

Family engagement work is complex. Because of the multi-faceted nature of the work, it is not possible for just one person to bear the responsibility of engaging families at an organization or school. While we often find that there may be only one person with "family engagement" officially included in his or her title, engaging families truly is the work of everyone involved in the organization.

The idea of family engagement as a shared responsibility becomes even more obvious when we reflect on the integral importance of relationships to engagement efforts. Families interact with multiple staff members throughout their day; they may drop off their child with an aide or front desk administrator, receive a phone call from the child's teacher during the day, and then get an email from the food service staff to confirm their child's food allergy. Each of those individuals helps to shape the family's path of engagement.

Shared understanding

Families and community members each have their own ideas about the responsibilities that are included in their roles. Organizations and staff dedicated to children's learning and development often serve as the intermediary between all the partners involved in engagement efforts. Thus it can fall to staff to help bring everyone to a shared understanding. For example, families may need support in understanding the value they bring to the organization or school—especially if they have never been involved in such an in-depth way before. Likewise, staff may need support as they explore their responsibilities to the overall goals of family engagement, and how those fit within the other duties of their job.

Before we can get to the discussion of who does what, and when, it is important to have a shared understanding of what the organization's overall goals are in terms of family engagement. These goals are often tied to some form of partnership that leads to improved child or family outcomes, but may have some variation between organizations.

Partnering, for example, can mean different things to different people, yet it is a critical component of effective engagement.

As an organization, it is important to be on the same page about what partnering looks like in real interactions, within the context of your community. Partnering around decision making, for instance, can look very different from planning a community event together—even when the same players are involved.

You may notice that some individuals are more open to partnering in certain scenarios than others. Take, for example, a staff member who doesn't believe that families should influence their child's learning in the organization, but is perfectly

Setting the stage

Your organization holds the responsibility for preparing both staff and families for partnership in tasks that require working together. If partnership is forced when partners are not ready, it can backfire, potentially creating big rifts in the community. These rifts can have negative effects, not only on the organization, but on the unity of the community as a whole, which can hamper efforts to engage in the future.

Researchers and authors of "Mise en Place: Setting the Stage for Thought and Action" note strong parallels here to setting the stage for student success in educational settings. When the environment around students is prepped to support their learning—psychological and physical considerations are taken into account before a task begins—behavior and performance will increase.

Setting the stage for engagement might include activities that foster the skills for effective group work, including how to address emotionally-charged interactions. Learning these skills in a collaborative learning setting, that includes both staff and families, can lay the foundation for a common operating lens. Having opportunities for casual gatherings where staff and families get to know each other will also support the development of positive working relationships.

willing to plan a community dinner with families. You may have to support the motivation of these individuals by making a connection between the value of the partnership around learning activities, and child outcomes or other goals they hold. Explicitly calling out the value of these interactions creates a shared understanding of what a deeper level of partnership actually looks like in specific and concrete ways.

Whatever the circumstances in your organization or school, it is up to you to continue to push the boundaries of what partnering with families and the community looks like in your organization. While it is easier to partner with someone that you like, it is not a critical component of partnering (though it does make it much more enjoyable). We encourage you to push yourselves to think beyond the ways you are currently sharing responsibility. Do you partner with families to plan learning activities or only community events? Are only those families who are a part of the formalized parent group in your community involved? The continuum we referred to in the introduction calls for us to continually move towards deeper partnerships with families.

reflection

How does your organization understand partnering with families?

What steps could you take to prepare the environment for optimal engagement?

Defining roles

The wide, varied definitions of family engagement also affect the views and interpretations of who is responsible for what. Depending on what definition your organization decides to adopt, different tasks and roles might be assigned to different parties. However your organization decides to define the work, there are several roles that are common across variations in implementation, both for families and staff.

Defining roles for staff

As we discussed in "Trust", staff bear many of the responsibilities for laying the groundwork for positive relationships with families through their everyday actions. Author Heidi Wachter suggests actions such as setting and respecting boundaries, talking about shared goals, keeping confidences, being accountable, acting with transparency, and having discussions in person. Underlying all of these is a common expectation that everyone will follow through on commitments, be good stewards of resources, show integrity, and hold others' best interests in mind.

Job descriptions that spell out specific skills, knowledge, tasks, goals, and assignments can set the stage for successful interactions, events, or activities. Everyone can have engagement responsibilities written into their job descriptions in some way or another. It can be helpful, especially when beginning a new practice, to flesh out your expectations in descriptions or contracts so that no one is surprised by the time they will be expected to spend on tasks related to engaging families.

While formalized job descriptions are helpful, the tasks that are listed in them, as in any job, do not begin to cover the entirety of work that you'll find yourself doing. In any organization that serves families, things pop up unexpectedly. It can be beneficial to talk through some of these possible scenarios—perhaps by reviewing examples of situations that have come up for other organizations in their family engagement work—to avoid surprises.

Talk with staff to see where they might visualize their strengths supporting the work, outside of their assigned roles. Conversations like these can serve as a reminder of the commitments that staff members have, and can help the organization develop a successful approach to tackling those unexpected roles and situations. It also helps to reduce frustration by helping staff to anticipate additional work or sudden challenges. Letting people self-select roles also allows them to get creative. You might find an unknown talent in someone that will push your initiatives further than you imagined.

When staff and other volunteers choose their roles, as they relate to family engagement, it is important to document those choices and let everyone know who is responsible for what. This allows for coordination of tasks, as well as accountability for those who have taken on tasks outside of their given roles. Not only that, posting roles can highlight the deep level of engagement by staff in the process, as others see how many people are working on various initiatives or events. We will dive deeper into families' roles further on in this chapter, but highlighting family and community members who have taken on a role, in the same way that you highlight staff involvement, integrates them in the process, and communicates their importance as well.

from the field

Once you establish a culture that values engaging families, it will start to speak for itself. Matt Arend, principal at Sigler Elementary in Plano, Texas, found that, as the school's reputation for successfully and intentionally engaging families grew, job candidates became more attracted to the school. Over time, families started to seek out the school because they wanted to be a part of this family-focused community. Arend estimates that nearly 20 percent of his students are transfers whose families choose to drive from other parts of the city because they believe in the work the school is doing to partner with families.

At times, we may slip into the mind-set that if we invite families to events or meetings, then it is their responsibility to show up and engage. While that may hold some truth, inviting isn't the end of our responsibility. Once parents arrive, staff are responsible for making parents feel welcome by conversing with them, and providing them with the information they need, as well as the context for that information. This will increase the likelihood that families who show up feel valued and a part of the team. We wouldn't throw a new colleague into a meeting without giving them some sort of background information they needed—so why do that to parents?

Being able to clearly articulate why families are invited and what their roles are is also important to avoid frustration and confusion. Before any information is given, the context for the invitation is critical to set everyone up for success. If you invited families to simply listen to information that is being given, let them know that. If you invited families in order to gather their feedback or opinions, or if you want them to participate in discussions, let them know that too. If these expectations for everyone's roles are not clear it can lead both staff and families to feel like they did not get the outcomes they wanted. If roles are clearly defined, you can set up both families and staff for productive conversations and interactions.

Just as it is important to identify what responsibilities lie with staff, it is equally important to identify what their roles are not. Staff may struggle with identifying where their responsibility ends, especially as they begin to be more aware of the needs of the families they serve. In a 2018 PATNC family engagement survey, one parent educator suggested that programs train staff on boundaries from the start. "I have often seen new staff become enmeshed in families' problems and try to solve problems for them, rather than educate and empower families. Likewise, veteran staff can fall into the same pattern when their knowledge and experience allow them to take charge, again disempowering families." Help staff to identify where their responsibilities end, and how to avoid unintentionally disempowering families.

Challenges for staff

As most of you probably know, it is not always an easy transition to weave family engagement into responsibilities for staff. There are additional time commitments, new processes and procedures to learn, and often a shift to a whole new mind-set. These can be big asks of staff, on top of all of the other responsibilities that they already have.

It is important to acknowledge these feelings of concern that come with increased responsibility as real and valid. Simply stating that the school expects staff to interact positively with every family, or that they find a way to engage whenever convenient for the family, creates an oversimplified view of reality. Sometimes positive interactions require strategies. Timing of events and meetings requires a balance of both families' and staff's schedules outside of regular work hours.

Just as families' historical interactions with school might shape the way they interact with staff, staff's historical interactions with the community might bring up challenges to positive interaction as well. Prior history or outside relationships with an individual can make it more difficult to connect. For example, there may be a child in your school whose parent is a prominent politician in the community with whom you happen to disagree. Perhaps you find it difficult to see past their beliefs and interact with them as the parent of this child.

Whatever the circumstance, leadership may need to step in and help staff work to identify what success looks like in these moments. It might be that a staff member and family who do not get along are able to be cordial, if not friendly. Understand that any growth, no matter how small, can alter future interactions for the better.

Role reversal

Take a moment to put yourself in the shoes of parents who are first-time participants in an advisory board. They may be on the sidelines in a room full of staff who all know each other and are socializing before the meeting. A few staff might say hello, but then move on to others in the room. When the meeting starts, they are given an agenda, but some of the words and phrases are unfamiliar to them.

During the meeting, terminology that they have not heard before is used, but everyone else seems to understand. They feel uncomfortable with their lack of knowledge on the topic. As staff contribute to the discussion, it may feel like almost everyone else in the room knows what is going on except them.

As the meeting wraps up, the parents slip out quietly without interacting with staff, who are still socializing. How motivated would you be to come back to the next meeting if that were your experience?

By putting ourselves in the shoes of those families we hope to engage, we can begin to answer key questions and reduce common barriers that often stop them from fully participating. Sometimes we need to step back and ask not only how can we help, but also how we might be making it harder for families, despite our best efforts.

By supporting staff through challenges and encouraging them to focus on the small impacts of positive interactions, you can begin to see small shifts in culture. Just as with any challenging situation, when staff feel supported and acknowledged, they are more likely to try (even when it is difficult).

Providing staff with concrete support for engagement ideas, such as research or examples, will offer a rationale for implementation that might not be obvious in

Mingling roles

Breaking apart traditional notions of turf and ownership can make it easier for family engagement partnerships to thrive. For example, when planning for an event, we can reassign tasks that have traditionally fallen to staff to families instead. This can create a sense of teamwork among staff, families, and community members. Some of these responsibilities include:

- **Securing a room.** While this might seem like something a staff member needs to do, technology can facilitate scheduling requests, or someone can connect with a staff member who schedules rooms.

- **Identifying the topic, speaker, or activity.** It can feel daunting to always come up with topics—let families help!

- **Arranging for supplies and food.** Free online sign-up sites have proliferated in recent years that allow anyone to coordinate and track what is needed.

- **Spreading the word.** Both friendly verbal invitations from peers and formal write-ups distributed via the organization's database of contacts are important.

- **Welcoming at the start of an event and gathering feedback at the end.** Feedback might be more open and honest if collected by someone from the community.

their own work yet, and can help move through feelings of resistance they might have. When they know the outcomes of other, similar measures, along with the potential these changes have to make their jobs easier, staff will be motivated to push through the emotional challenges and stress that are a natural part of the process of change.

Defining roles for families

Although families don't usually enter into partnerships with organizations by way of job descriptions, our expectations for them are often remarkably similar to those described for staff. If we have certain expectations for families, it can be beneficial to lay them out just as we do for staff. The Portland, Maine, Board of Public Education does this by publishing a policy that lays out what the board, district, and schools will do to foster family engagement—followed by a list of what families can do on their end. These expectations include: advocating for their child when they identify that support is needed; keeping the school informed about everything from contact information to changes in home life that may impact the child's learning; being receptive to updates from the school about what and how students are learning; and volunteering when possible. These examples are just a few ways that might be identified for families to engage.

Once again, how you express these expectations matters as well. Using directive words like "should" and "have to" can take away feelings of partnership if these expectations are not decided upon together with the families. Listing families expectations next to those for staff can also prevent them from appearing one-sided, making it clear that there are expectations for everyone.

Families may not be used to having input that is valued and central to decisions for the organization. When starting to include family input, it is important to be clear about where you expect contributions to be made, and ultimately what decisions will be made by whom in order to avoid confusion. It is sure to create frustration when participants believe they will be a part of a decision, only to learn when the time comes that their input did not actually influence the decision after all.

Spreading the word

The best way to get buy-in? Talk about the great work that is happening! It is the responsibility of all those who believe in the power of family engagement to talk about it—both their own experiences and the growing body of research. Personal stories reinforce what research says by pointing out the benefits in real life. Researchers at the Global Family Research Project have noted that highlighting positive experiences and moments of growth can go a long way. Those who might be skeptical of the work because of the time and effort it takes may be more likely to believe stories of success when they are told by peers, or by families themselves.

Getting families to tell their stories about what engagement means to them is vitally important—not only to staff, but also to other families and the community. Engaged families who see the benefits on a personal level are the best positioned to bring in other families. These personal relationships are a powerful way to spread the impact.

Spreading the word about the benefits of family engagement must go beyond the organization, into the community, and also beyond the community. We know that family engagement, while it can be cheap, is rarely free. Efforts that require extra staff time also require money. Implementing new strategies and pushing for change in policies takes time and effort. By talking about their experiences, organizations can help others navigate the unknown, and help them to see why it is worth it.

"Family engagement is one of the most important aspects of our program because without families involved in our program, we wouldn't exist. It is important to meet all families where they are and try to help them meet their goals while also helping us reach our grant-required goals."

– 2018 PATNC family engagement survey

Though we are sure it doesn't come as a shock, there is rarely any extra money lying around waiting to be spent on family engagement efforts. Families and staff telling their stories of success can boost funding for initial efforts, as well as demonstrate the long term effectiveness of family engagement. Each of these ensures that family engagement work is allocated additional resources when it comes time for budget considerations. We have seen the impacts of spreading the word as more funding is allocated for family engagement at federal and state levels in recent years.

The more well-versed everyone is in talking about family engagement in your organization, the more likely it is to be funded. Staff and families are your best advocates, but they may need support to fill in gaps of information, or to find the right wording. Finding opportunities for families and staff to tell their stories not only supports the organization, but also empowers them as leaders in the initiative.

from the field

A parent educator shared this view of the dual responsibilities she and her families hold in an early childhood home visiting program: "To me, family engagement means developing a rapport with the families that our program serves so that they want to continue to engage with us and actively participate in the program. By this I mean that they are not merely passive recipients of the information and services that we provide, but rather buy into the process and participate fully in the planning, delivery, and assessment of program services. They are invested in the process of participating and have developed a relationship with both their parent educator and the program itself."

Trainings to develop storytelling and advocacy skills can be another great (and fun) way to incorporate dual learning opportunities for staff and families to learn side-by-side. These communication skills are also beneficial to staff and families in other roles, and can add to their credentials as they move into leadership or other positions. Armed with knowledge and information, families will become your best advocates, and staff will be more equipped to build buy-in—both inside the organization and out.

reflection

How are you equipping staff and families to tell their stories of engagement?

Organizational responsibilities

As each staff and family member has a unique role to play in family engagement efforts, each school or organization also has its own responsibilities to fulfill. Integrating these duties into the policies and practices of the organization will go a long way towards improving your overall ability to engage families.

Getting into the community

"If anxiety and mistrust can prevent families from walking in the doors of a school, then it is our mutual responsibility to engage them outside of the school."

– Successful Innovations Inc., *A Correlation/Crosswalk of Family Engagement On Demand to the Dual Capacity Building Framework*

Many engagement efforts have traditionally occurred within the walls of a school or center. This requires families to leave their comfort zone and enter into a space that is more familiar to—and controlled by—staff. Even if staff do their best to make the space reflect the community, it may continue to be unfamiliar and uncomfortable.

This atmosphere can make families reluctant to engage. Feeling like you are an "outsider" in a strange environment is not conducive to productive thinking and learning! Think about this as you plan activities and meetings where you want families to engage. Ask families what would be most comfortable for them, and take their answers into consideration when planning.

As someone who is coordinating engagement efforts, your end goal may be to get the highest participation you can from families. Numbers may not be the best metric for determining the level of engagement, but they are a common one required by many funders and agencies. Meeting families where they are, and not always expecting them to come to you, can significantly impact the number of families who are both able and willing to show up. Remember all the factors we have explored that can lead to families feeling more welcome at events or more comfortable having a conversation. Taking events into the community, varying times and days, and other considerations discussed in "Accessibility" can increase the participation of families overall.

Gathering data to inform the field

For a long time, family engagement work was overlooked, in part due to the difficulty in collecting quantitative data, or even determining what appropriate data points were. Even today, there is not a set standard of outcomes or tools that really measures family engagement, although there are many tools that attempt to measure specific aspects of engagement. It is an ever-evolving process that relies on the people in the field, like you, to continue to add to the body of data that supports the work!

Each organization has a responsibility to the larger field to develop strategies, events, and initiatives based upon data that you gather from your community and the families you serve. This data may be quantitative, from formal data-collection efforts such as surveys or interviews. More often than not, author Lynda Tredway points out, it comes in the form of conversations and qualitative data collection.

The conversations that happen every day between staff, families, and the community are rich with information about what your families need, what engagement should look like, and what is making a difference. As noted in *Principal Leadership*, establishing formalized processes for gathering feedback—

both through wide-reaching strategies like community learning exchanges, and through more intimate measures such as one-on-one conversations—will help your organization tell the story of how families engage with you.

Once you've gathered data around engagement, both the successes and the challenges, it's essential that you share what you've learned. Your experiences are invaluable to other organizations, and sharing your trials and tribulations, as well as the information you've gathered, is crucial in pushing the work forward.

reflection

What are ways that you currently collect data from your community? Think about both quantitative and qualitative data collection methods.

What data are you missing that you would like to collect? What formats might yield additional data about your families or about outcomes that you are hoping to achieve?

Sharing responsibility

Throughout this chapter, we've explored some of the shared responsibilities and distinct roles within family engagement. We hope that, as you continue to reflect on each of the values in these chapters, you will start to clarify your role, and how you can best contribute moving forward.

We also hope that, if you are currently the "one" responsible for family engagement at your school or organization, you might find some relief in knowing that even if others aren't clearly assigned engagement duties in their job descriptions yet, they are still responsible for initiatives' success. It's not all up to you!

We encourage you to use this book and other resources to think about the ways in which you can realistically make an impact on the work, and be kind to yourself when you are taking on more than you can or should have to. Find your team, lean in, and move the work forward.

Responsibility

Responsibility happens at both a personal and an organizational level. It includes stewardship of resources, following through on commitments, showing integrity, and holding others' best interests in mind.

moving forward

There are many aspects to responsibility. Take a moment to reflect on the previous chapter and think about which ideas, strategies, or pieces of responsibility are strongest, and which require growth.

> **Defining roles for staff**
> **Challenges for staff**
> **Defining roles for families**

> **Getting into the community**
> **Gathering data to inform the field**

We're strong on this:

We're so-so at this:

We're working on it:

Generosity

To give freely and kindly; not to be attached to material possessions; to be generous. These are common phrases you might find in one of the many definitions of generosity. In fact, generosity is so important that it is considered a virtue by many religions and spiritual organizations. While that might seem a bit lofty for talking about family engagement, we have observed a clear connection to success when initiatives are infused with this value.

Engaging and partnering with families requires a lot of giving. Giving of time, giving of resources, giving of knowledge; many "gifts" that often come with no rewards or recognition. Families, staff, volunteers, and so many others give huge amounts of time and talent to make sure that they are all creating the best possible space for children to learn and grow.

The meaning of generosity

Although we have provided a few words related to the concept of generosity, what it truly means to be generous varies from one individual to the next, and from one situation to another. In this work, providing opportunities for individuals to be generous in the ways that work best for them, and accepting their generosity in return, is deeply important.

Often individuals have set ideas and opinions about how much people should give. When others don't give as much as we expect, it can create situations where people are disappointed, or even angry. This can apply to both staff and families. When we talk about generosity, we're not talking about completing the tasks written in a job description, or expectations spelled out for families in a handbook. We are talking about the efforts that go above and beyond those baseline expectations.

Generosity, in the context of family engagement, embodies many other traits, such as open-mindedness, flexibility, tolerance, and warmth. Although there are ways to demonstrate our generosity that are tangible, we are also referring to an overall attitude. Generosity might look like embracing a certain way of looking at things that includes assuming best intentions, and giving others the benefit of the doubt.

Gauging readiness

Deciding to become more intentional about embracing the value of generosity will require commitment from everyone involved in the organization. As we grow in willingness to share in a multitude of ways, we also commit to maintaining a generous mind-set, by accepting generosity from others who give it in various ways as well. This is not a one-time decision, but rather a commitment we renew daily. Because of the effort that can be required, it is important that we feel ready to commit to the shift in mind-set, both individually and as an organization. Determining what "ready" means to everyone within your organization is important, since the whole effort requires all hands on deck. One person may be eager to dive right in and embrace generosity in its entirety, but the next person may barely be ready to dip a toe into the water. There are many assessment tools that can help you evaluate readiness for engagement efforts overall, with more coming out all the time; you may need to do some exploring, or create your own tool to find one that fits your needs.

Gauging readiness for engagement is as complex as engagement itself, and requires looking at many facets. It includes both looking at how open one is to accepting what families are offering, and being able to share one's own resources of time and talent. Readiness happens at different paces for each individual within the organization, and varies within an individual as well. A person may be willing to be generous with their own time, but not yet ready to accept families' contributions. It helps to remember that assessing readiness doesn't have to be a big, scary thing. It is not a test to pass—instead, it is simply a way to raise awareness of where everyone stands so that you can position the next initiative or strategy accordingly.

If readiness is low, professional development or education for staff and families about what family engagement means to your school or organization may be a necessary first step. You might also find that you need to take a deeper look at your own preconceptions and thoughts about how families fit into the puzzle.

We are all more likely to stay connected and continue to give our time and skills if we see that our generosity is well received and used.

Readiness is a process. It requires continually revisiting willingness for each new strategy or stage as you move into it. As you grow, the methods you choose will change. Eventually you will get the chance to try that ambitious new initiative that you've been waiting to implement, but it just wasn't the right time until now. Knowing what your partners are ready for greatly increases the odds of success.

Staff readiness

You may find yourselves with families who are ready to help and lead however they can, but your staff isn't ready to let them, or ready to be equally generous with their own time and efforts. The opposite can also be true; staff are ready but families are not yet. Remember that a successful partnership needs all parties, even if they are at different points on the continuum. Moving forward cannot happen if only one partner is being generous or if only one partner is making an effort. This is a direct route to frustration and burnout.

It's OK not to be completely ready as an organization to fully partner with families—no one is ever completely ready for something that is unknown. However, it can be helpful to have a foundation built on the expectation that generosity and an open mind-set are the goal. Moving towards these goals offers opportunities for growth. Just as we ask families to grow through their relationship with us, it is not unreasonable for them to expect growth from us. One parent educator summed it up this way on a PATNC survey: "If everything is a walk in the park and sunshine and rainbows, then we, as practitioners, are missing something. Not to sound as if things must be gloomy, but each human on this earth has room for growth. Learning through our experiences isn't always pleasant, but if we support one another, we can build resilience, and the families we serve can build resilience."

Reflecting on partners

A partner might be the organization as a whole. It might be an entire family—including family members other than parents. It might be another organization in the community. Remember that not everyone will be at the same place in their path towards partnership, and that is completely normal! Part of the challenge in partnership is figuring out how to best move forward at a pace and in a way that does not leave anyone behind, and allows everyone to grow together.

A generous mind-set

A shift towards a more generous mind-set in the context of family engagement can mean a lot of things. For one, it can mean shifting the focus or conversation away from what we can "get" from families, to wondering how we might be able to give to families. A generous attitude is also related to a strengths-based lens, in that we practice being open-minded to the ways that we can continue to grow in partnership. We become more flexible, looking to what families are already contributing, and finding ways to build on these existing possibilities. We become more generous in the ways we're willing to extend ourselves and our thinking for the benefit of all.

Be open to other paths into engagement

Although we have talked a lot about families as partners in decision making, for most of them, this level of partnership is not the initial entry point into a partnership with your organization. There may be many reasons for this—families may not be ready, staff are not ready, or the organization as a whole is not ready. However, just because families are not contributing to decisions, for whatever reason, does not mean they are not contributing to the organization in a multitude of ways—some more obvious than others.

We have reflected on the many strengths of families throughout this book, and examining these strengths can help you to see where families are already contributing, or may easily do so if given an opportunity. Looking to these strengths, and where they might be used to push the organization forward, is one way to begin shifting mind-sets to be able to see all the ways that families can share with your organization or school.

At the very least, families bring with them their love and passion for their children. In order to capitalize on the energy and passion that parents bring to the table, it is our role to create spaces that elicit families' ideas and channel their energy towards positive change. We can all agree that there is no one-size-fits-all plan to fix any of the issues that exist within our communities and schools. The knowledge that parents have, not only about their child, but about the community as well, can shift your organization into a highly functional space—but only if you let it.

You might explore how families might help, or are helping, with small decisions. Find ways to recognize their leadership in ways they might not have thought about, from their parenting roles at home, to activities in their communities.

Research from the Search Institute shows that professionals sometimes view families that lack material resources as having nothing to contribute to partnerships. They are more likely to be viewed as passive consumers at best, or as people who will show up only if incentives are offered. These stereotypes can foster an atmosphere where disproportionate economic resources can leave some families feeling inadequate, regardless of their other desires to engage.

Even when trying to look for strengths in families you might find yourself thinking, "we have to drag parents to get involved in school. I can't imagine how we can do anything else to bring them in." You might be right—there might not be an obvious outpouring of families knocking at your door asking to be engaged directly. But you might also have a group of moms who talk on the curb outside after dropping their kids off at school each morning, who might be willing to do that talking inside at a parent café if you hold one. You might have parents who always

> You and your staff do not have to be the experts who orchestrate ways for families to be involved. In fact, you are not the experts—families are. Use every opportunity to show families you believe in their capacity to be the experts in their own hopes, goals, needs, and wants.

have a suggestion for you when you see them about how the school could be doing things better. Pull those voices in, even if they are critical, and provide channels for them to lend their voice or time in ways that both empower them and build up your school.

In every community there are also families who are unsure, or do not yet know the avenue to engage. Because some families are not yet ready to speak their thoughts out loud, or do not feel comfortable in the space, think about other ways that you might support them that feel authentic. These families might be your best-kept secret. Some families prefer to give in-kind, by bringing needed items for an event. Others may wish to be more hands-on, and contribute to décor, or set up spaces around the building. Could they provide food at a potluck event? Distribute flyers via text message to other families they know? Finding ways for families to demonstrate how they can give is so important.

Be creative and think about the many ways people might be comfortable contributing as you brainstorm opportunities. One district hosts what it calls a "superpower summit"—a resource fair where families offer their skills and knowledge, and the organization matches its needs to the volunteers' "superpowers."

from the field

Parent educator Ann Miller experienced a particularly simple—and successful—community-building initiative at the center where she works, in a neighborhood north of Chicago: a parent-run toy-lending library. Fueled by donations from families, the library sanitized all toys before handing them out, but otherwise had no strict rules. "We gave no specific due dates. If a toy comes back, great. If not, great," Miller said. Ahead of the winter holiday season, the center promoted popular commercial toys and homemade playthings in a "toy hall of fame" that showcased toys families might want to choose for their children.

Miller believes one reason for the lending library's success is that it engaged families in smaller, more manageable chunks of time and effort. It also let them decide what and when to share.

Rolling with the setbacks

We often hear from service providers, staff, and teachers that they ask families what they would like to happen to support their ability to engage, but don't get any responses. Others may get responses, but when they try to implement what families have suggested, the strategy is still unsuccessful— no parents show up. This can be incredibly frustrating. In these moments, it is tempting to give up and not ask families for input again.

As difficult as it may be, take these moments and look for the learning. What could have gone differently? What unanticipated barrier came up that prevented a family from participating? Was there a competing event in their neighborhood? There are so many questions to ask when things don't go as planned, but asking them can lead you to growth in the next attempt. Avoid looking at these moments as personal failures, even if it might feel that way sometimes.

As you look back on an unsuccessful attempt at engagement, think about how you might gather information in ways that support your growth as well. For example, you might have relationships with parents who will honestly share about what could have been different. Prepare for this conversation intentionally, as the language you use needs to be productive, and not put people on the defensive. Consider these two examples:

> *Why didn't you come to the event last night?*

> *What could we have done differently to increase attendance at last night's event?*

Notice that the wording in the second example shifts the focus off of the individual and onto the organization. It also shifts the questions from asking what personally made them not come—which can lead to feelings of embarrassment or shame—to asking about why others might not have come. This allows the individual to work his or her own reasoning into the conversation as a hypothetical. It also provides the family with a role, as an informant on what is happening in the community.

As a bonus, if they see their suggestions implemented, they are more likely to show up in the future.

Parent educators who visit families in their homes operate in two spheres of power: their employer's and the family's. When asked in a 2018 PATNC family engagement survey about what works and what doesn't within family engagement efforts, they shared the following from their unique vantage points:

"When a decision has to be made, it seems to be better if it is a team decision. The saying is true that two heads are better than one. It can be valuable to get more than one perspective."

"Making decisions needs to be a group effort... decision making doesn't work if there aren't choices, if the parents aren't involved, or if the parents don't feel like you are listening to their concerns."

"When home visitors take the families' perspectives and insights into consideration, it helps create a positive partnership. It does not work if a home visitor takes power, or an authority presence in the relationship."

"It works when we are all good listeners, and truly believe that everyone has something important to offer to the partnership. It doesn't work if you bring people to the table but the leader already has their ideas or agenda and others feel like they are not being listened to, or that their ideas are not important because they are never acted on. It is important to be clear about how the decisions are made and who was involved in making them, but also encouraging feedback—and truly wanting it."

"What works: making decisions with families' input because they matter and they actually have great ideas once you have received input. They like to see that they were considered."

"Families need to be asked before the decisions are even considered. More than once, I gave a thumbs down to an idea that others wisely did not let go of, and they produced phenomenal outcomes."

Being generous with power

Partnerships are all about give and take. They require a balance in order for everyone to feel like they are getting what they need from the partnership—and are inspired to continue to be a part of it. This social exchange also includes the sharing of power, which can be tricky to navigate.

Think of all of the ways that we have looked at power thus far—in building trust, respecting others' strengths, taking responsibility, making decisions—and you'll quickly recognize how significant a role power plays in partnerships. We will continue to reference the sharing of power in the following chapters as well, because it is critical to forming sustainable partnerships.

As educators or staff of an organization, you have power by default. Families also have inherent power. Parents have power in their families, and they have power in their level of knowledge about the community and their children.

Finding ways to share power means navigating your unique relationships to decide what shared power looks like within them. Relinquishing some power or sense of control, to allow for more balanced partnerships in your organization, reflects a generous approach and a generous mind-set.

reflection

Where do you see an opportunity to pull in voices from families who might not engage in the "expected" ways, or during the structured opportunities for engagement?

How can your organization demonstrate generosity by opening up processes for gathering input and shared decision making?

Family giving: special considerations

While we can mandate that our staff build family engagement efforts and actions into their work, we cannot do the same for families. There are certain exceptions—for example, some organizations have requirements for the amount of time or money that is donated by participants—but even then it is difficult, if not impossible, to mandate engagement. When families are engaged, it is because they want to be, because they see the value for their child and the children in the community when they become part of the process. As families become more engaged, we will encounter amazing benefits as an organization, while simultaneously working through some growing pains.

Getting something you didn't ask for

Getting to a point where you and your school or organization feels ready to fully receive from families can be extremely challenging. There may be times you are given something that you didn't ask for or didn't particularly want, like something you perceive as criticism.

There are countless examples of families who rally together in communities to fight for the right to have a say in their child's education or care, and donate a great deal of time and energy to the cause. Some might view this as disruptive,

Gathering input from families

Experts at the Harvard Family Research Project argue that, when used together, the strategies in human-centered design and the mind-set of design thinking allow all stakeholders a structured way to give input on decisions and direction, to ensure that the end product is both usable and useful for the end user. Both strategies capitalize on family input by implementing workshops and conversations that give families a space to reflect on their hopes and dreams, as well as provide a real view into their struggles and challenges, to come up with solutions to problems that work for them.

Providing these opportunities takes the guesswork out for teachers and staff; they are able to hear directly from parents in a structured way. These methods of gathering data and making decisions come from the world of design at Stanford's d.School, and global design and innovation firm IDEO, and are being implemented in fields from social work and education to health and information technology to create more sustainable solutions to all sorts of challenges. They are discussed more in the chapter "Initiative".

especially when the parents are challenging the status quo. Alternatively, we could choose to see this as a commitment to securing their child's future by seeking a place to engage.

As mentioned in the introduction to this book, family and community advocacy is one of the great benefits that can grow out of family engagement. From a perspective of generosity, families advocating for their children represents a success, as it indicates so many positive outcomes for families and organizations alike. However, if this advocacy includes what we perceive as criticism, it is easy to fall into the mind-set that this involvement is negative. Keep in mind that advocacy is an important component of family giving, and it powerfully reflects the dedication and drive of families.

Picture for a moment a group of families advocating for more voice in an underperforming school district. Regardless of their message or method, they have a few things in common. First, they are giving time towards their cause in an organized manner. They are meeting with other families, showing up at meetings at school, and perhaps outside of school. They are connecting with others by building relationships, motivating them to show up, organizing a time and place to meet, and maybe even providing transportation if necessary. Each of these tasks requires generosity of time and effort—and when partnered with your staff, their skills could be driving your organization toward success.

What if, instead of seeing these parents who are "rocking the boat" as a problem, we see them as an opportunity? Imagine how that passion for and perspective on their children can shape the work you and your organization or school are trying to do.

These gatherings and conversations that families are having about change they'd like to see are windows into the needs of families. They can be wonderful opportunities to open up productive conversations that explore shared goals and unite efforts to make change. Taking the time to dig into concerns, instead of viewing them as battles to be won, might open doors to build relationships you never thought were possible.

Overcommitment

At times, we may encounter very involved families that lie on the far end of the engagement continuum. Parents who show up to everything, always going above and beyond any request, may seem like a family engagement dream. It can be tempting to rely on them often because they get the job done. There are a couple of things to watch for in this scenario. Be sure to ask yourself whether their quick enthusiasm is eclipsing others who might also be willing and able to do the work but are less likely to be the first to volunteer. Also question whether it's possible that their dedication has become overcommitment—requiring the time and energy that is usually only fair to expect from a paid employee. It's possible for volunteers to say yes more often than they should, putting other commitments ahead of themselves and their families.

In settings like elementary schools, where parents tend to have multiple children over a span of several grades, those who jump into every opportunity will build up a wealth of knowledge—all of which they will take with them when their youngest child advances to the next school. They also tend to get comfortable (some might say entrenched) in familiar routines, making them less likely to consider new ideas or ways of doing things. This can be daunting to other would-be volunteers and newcomers to the family engagement space at your organization.

reflection

How are you creating spaces where families are welcome to give whatever they have to offer, whether that is time, talent, or simply presence?

What might you do to elicit ideas from families about how they might like to give?

Is your organization preserving spaces for newcomers?

Generosity between organizations

We have spent much of our time talking about family engagement at an organizational or school level, but we recognize that family engagement extends to the community as well. In fact, various researchers confirm that strategies that are implemented across an entire community can be very impactful.

Community engagement can support the individual organization in creating sustainable family engagement. Many of the families that you work with are also probably engaged in other spaces or have contact with other organizations nearby. Maybe they have a student at the elementary school and one at the local preschool. That family is now trying to navigate two different systems of engagement if they are not connected.

Creating systems of engagement that cross sectors and communities can reduce the overlap of work that has already been done and create a consistent experience for families. While not every organization or school will have the same places and ways for families to engage, gauging if they are willing to combine efforts is a strong start for increasing engagement all around.

Think about that family that has two children in two different schools. Mom and dad might be very engaged in the preschool, which has actively tried to partner with them and pull them into the process of moving the child through preschool.

Sharing resources

Any new experience is easier to navigate if there is a template to follow. Many organizations and schools in the U.S. understand this, and are sharing a wealth of resources to support others in their journey towards successful engagement. After you have used this book to help you lay the foundations of what engagement looks like to your organization, you will be better prepared to think critically about how to pick up these strategies, and how to adapt them to fit within your community.

One challenge for many schools and organizations is answering the question of how to evaluate or measure engagement. Evaluation and measurement tools exist in multiple places online, and can be tailored to individual needs. Boston Public Schools is one example of an organization that shares these resources online, as part of its *Interactive Rubric of Effective Teaching*. Under the third standard, family engagement, it offers resources and next steps for teachers who want to help the district move from proficient to exemplary.

When their older child enters elementary school, the parents attempt to engage in the same way they had in preschool, and find they are not welcome. This may result in the parents reducing the ways in which they are engaged in the preschool for their younger child because they no longer see an avenue for growing with the child, or are simply frustrated.

While this could also result in a family that that pushes for engagement opportunities even further in the elementary school, you never know what might be sacrificed if this family disengages. Taking the time to weave experiences across schools and sectors can enhance everyone's ability to work together. This is true across healthcare and education, and even in jobs where families might work in your community. Reaching out to create partnerships across these bridges also will demonstrate to families that you are attempting to understand their experiences and create a way to reduce their barriers to engagement.

reflection

How might you share resources or information about family engagement you've learned with other organizations that might be beneficial to them?

What organizations in your community might you be able to connect with to share strategies and ideas for engaging families?

Attitudes and actions

Although generosity is a word with plenty of positive connotations, it does not follow that practicing generosity on a daily basis is easy. This value asks all partners in family engagement to give—not only of our resources, like our time and energy—but to extend ourselves in the effort of building a generous way of thinking and acting. Be generous in your approach, especially when evaluating readiness, or the shortcomings of your organization. Adopting an attitude of tolerance and flexibility will help you weather the challenges you face as you partner with families on the journey of engagement. Remember, it's about striving for mutual growth, not perfection.

Generosity

When generosity infuses partnerships, there is a spirit of sharing—whether it's time, resources, information, power, or authority.

moving forward

There are many aspects to generosity. Take a moment to reflect on the previous chapter and think about which ideas, strategies, or pieces of generosity are strongest, and which require growth.

> **Staff readiness**
> **Be open to other paths into engagement**
> **Rolling with the setbacks**
> **Being generous with power**

> **Getting something you didn't ask for**
> **Overcommitment**
> **Attitudes and actions**

We're strong on this:

We're so-so at this:

We're working on it:

Accessibility

Accessibility is critical. What may seem on the surface to be disengagement might actually be that a family simply does not have access to what they need to engage. Barriers to engagement are as common as they are varied, and while we might not be able to eliminate them all, organizations can do their best to reduce their impact and increase families' ability to get, and stay, engaged.

Professionals and families alike often report that transportation, language, location, timing, and childcare are some of the most common barriers to engagement. These are very real factors that prevent families from coming to the table, and we'll explore each of them in this chapter. While these are all important, they are not the only aspects of accessibility to consider.

"Obviously, as we all know, language is a barrier. Transportation can be a barrier. The lack of trust between families and the school system is a barrier. And one that oftentimes I don't hear enough about—but I believe I have identified as a barrier—is that we don't see our families as true partners in very honest terms."

– **Salvador Romero,** *Coordinator of Family and Community Engagement for Harrisonburg City Public Schools*

Accessibility is so much more than the physical logistics of arriving at a place or participating in an event. Try putting yourself in a parent's position and reflect on all of the factors that might make an event or meeting inaccessible to you. For starters, perhaps you don't feel emotionally safe—having conversations about our children can make us feel vulnerable. You might have to let people in on challenges that your family is experiencing, or be open about the fact that you don't understand what the information that is being shared with you means. You might not participate because you don't have the information you need to be actively engaged; maybe you don't know all the details of an event, or you're not sure of the topic of conversation. Maybe you understand what the topic is, but don't feel like you know enough about it to fully engage. Perhaps you have a vision or hearing impairment and you know that the supports you need won't be available. These, plus countless other reasons, can also be true for families. How we address these barriers determines whether or not families engage with us. In addition to the factors that impede access to organizations, families' desires are also competing: resting after a long day at work, family time after a day apart, or even emotional protection from vulnerable conversations. If there are obstacles that families have to overcome

Harrisonburg Public Schools came up with a creative way to address two of the most common barriers—time and transportation—by taking their school's engagement programming to the families. Through an innovative partnership with a large employer in the area, Salvador Romero, the Family Engagement Coordinator of his district, was able to bring opportunities to families to engage with school, right at their workplace.

"We look at best practices in the field, obviously, but we also look at our own practices and our own challenges, and often our families can't come because time is of the essence. They get out of work late, they come tired, and their time is very limited. I strategically spoke with [the employer] and proposed that I would come and do workshops for their employees, who are our families. The proposal was basically that I would come, and we would provide workshops based on what they needed, so the families could be more engaged in their kids' educations. I told them that we would do an initial survey, talk with people informally, and gather information and the data that we need. Then we would move forward by creating workshops there at the plant, in their native language, and tell the company that it would be wonderful if, as a company, they could commit to their employees, and pay them in order for them to attend our workshops. I go to the plant and do the presentations in Spanish, and I also have our database available. Families can ask questions about their kids' attendance, they can ask questions about their grades, and they can ask questions about what it looks like for them as they move forward in their high school career. Through the workshops, informal conversations with the families, and then by connecting them further with people within the schools, then they are becoming more involved in their kids' education. They can be much more supportive, and empowered to really be able to get there and ask the right questions."

that make it difficult to participate in conversations or activities with an organization, families might feel that engaging is not worth the trouble.

When the information and rationale for engagement are difficult to access, relationships with staff or other engaged families can provide motivation for families who are unsure if the benefits outweigh the costs.

In this chapter, we encourage you to think of accessibility in all its forms, psychological as well as physical. We explore both kinds of common roadblocks to families' access—and offer examples of how forward-thinking organizations have successfully tackled them.

Connecting with the organization

Being able to access the building physically is an important part of families' ability to engage, one that is addressed in legal requirements put forth by the Americans with Disabilities Act (ADA). However, just because one is able to enter does not mean the building or organization is fully accessible. The look and feel of the building when one walks in the door sets the tone for families to feel like they belong; a critical but often overlooked component of accessibility.

Welcome

Positive relationships are a critical factor in creating inviting, welcoming spaces that are comfortable for families to engage in. These environments foster engagement, and encourage families to show up and get involved. Relationships with staff and other families at the school can support families in feeling that they are wanted and not like an outsider in the organization. The simplest way to create a welcoming environment and make families feel as though they belong is to greet families as they arrive.

Schools have demonstrated that putting a person at the front door or at the bus line, who waves and says hello to every parent and child, can go a long way. On the first day of school in School District 189, in East St. Louis, Illinois, it has become an annual tradition for students and parents at nearly every school in the city to be met with high-fives from a line of volunteers. Local residents partner with the non-

Americans with Disabilities Act (ADA) Compliance

Some pieces of accessibility are mandated by law, as many of you are probably familiar with. While ADA compliance is often referenced, it is complex and often misunderstood. Compliance with the original law required physical spaces to be accessible to people with disabilities of all kinds—hearing, vision, and physical disabilities included. In 2010, the law was extended to offer compliance guidance regarding the internet, addressing further design elements. A complete list of compliance standards can be found on the ADA website, but a few things to consider include:

- **Entrances.** Are ramps and stairs easy for all people to use? Are doors wide enough for wheelchairs to fit through?

- **Signage.** What colors are used on signs? Are they able to be read from the appropriate distance?

- **Hallways.** Are they wide and clear enough for someone in a wheelchair or on crutches to get down?

- **Assistance.** Are there devices available to assist those with hearing or vision impairments? Are they in good working order?

- **Transportation.** If you are providing transportation to and from events, is everyone able to use it?

profit organization, Saving Black Minds, to organize the rallies. Efforts like these set the stage for engagement by making students and parents feel welcome and wanted from the first day they enter the building.

Over time, having staff outside buildings to greet families as they drop off children not only lets them know they are welcome, but also creates a space for building the relationships between staff and families that form the foundation for further engagement.

The welcome that begins outside of the school should continue once families walk in. Consider who families might interact with when they enter the front door of your building. The first person that families see plays an especially important role; administrative staff in offices and front desks are the starting point for relationships that the family will build. Ideally this person is warm and inviting—welcoming families with a smile and offering them the support they need. This first interaction makes the space emotionally accessible, and sets the tone for further engagement.

While first impressions matter, we all know that the front desk staff are not the only ones that families communicate with in your organization. How the entire staff interacts with families has a major influence on engagement, and we're not just talking about teachers and home visitors either. In a survey PATNC conducted in 2018, hundreds of respondents described the variety of people involved in their family engagement efforts. "Although my title is Family Engagement Specialist," wrote one respondent, "every staff member plays a role in engaging our parents—from our receptionist as the first face and impression for our families

from the field

The consequences of having an unwelcoming environment are highlighted by the story of a grandmother in Missouri. She took her granddaughter to preschool just one time, and has not been back since. She opts to send her husband instead, entirely due to the difficulty of her first interaction with the school. She recalled walking up to the door and struggling to get in. The buzzer was not working (or so she thought) and she could not open the door. After trying the door and buzzer for a few minutes, another parent walked up and buzzed right in, so she followed in behind. To add to her embarrassment and discomfort, she was not sure once she got in where she was supposed to go. No one at the office offered to help her, and people walked by without saying a thing, despite her very confused look. After she finally asked someone for directions, she delivered her granddaughter to her classroom and walked out, never to return. When asked what would have made that experience better she stated: "If anyone had reached out to help me, I would have felt less embarrassed and more willing to go back."

to our cook who provides nutritional information, and everyone in between." This theme appears consistently in conversations around efforts to improve family engagement. Whole-staff commitment to positive interactions with families goes a long way in making organizations emotionally accessible to families.

Whether they are aware of it or not, everyone in the organization is welcoming families—whether they're doing so poorly or well. In the absence of organization-wide awareness, and effort from each staff member in the creation of a welcoming environment, engagement efforts will suffer.

Engagement is everyone's job

The list of roles of people who are responsible for family engagement efforts is impressively long. If you're not thinking about these people as a part of your engagement team, you might want to start.

- Center directors
- Van drivers
- Home visitors
- Family support providers
- Parent policy council members
- Community liaisons
- Teachers
- Guidance counselors
- Title 1 specialists
- Volunteers
- Custodians
- Chamber of Commerce members
- Assistant principals
- Group facilitators
- Executive directors
- Therapists
- Paraprofessional classroom assistants
- Case managers
- Nurses
- Central intake clerks
- Fatherhood specialists
- Community health workers
- Bus monitors

Lightening and brightening

Welcoming includes more than the feeling a family has when they come into your space, it also includes the look and feel of the space itself. Design elements can go a long way in reflecting a welcoming atmosphere. Not only that but the physical space can reflect the unique and fun personality of the organization as well!

Take a walk around your building and all of its access points. Explore what the physical space looks like at each entrance. Most schools and organizations are in older buildings, or are designed to feel industrial, which can be cold and uninviting. While you might not be able to change the physical layout or shape of the building, think about how you might shift the feel of the space with things like paint and plants.

Using lamps and furniture can also support a visitor feeling like they are walking into a place that feels more like home, or a living space, than a factory floor. You might think about who is able to donate furniture to you, or where you could pick up an inexpensive sofa, so that redesign efforts do not become an overwhelming expense. You might ask families to design the space—it could be a wonderful opportunity to not only get to know the families, but find out what reflects a comfortable environment to them as well.

Signage

One of the first things that families see upon entering a building, or even before they get inside, is signage. Many of the signs that can be found outside schools and organizations are mass produced, and probably look pretty similar to each other. Take a moment to read the signs that are posted around your building. Are they welcoming and cheerful? Do they offer messages that indicate that you think someone is doing something wrong and they need a reminder to do right? For example, compare these two signs that might be hanging outside of your building's entrance:

"Welcome to our school. In order to make sure that your child and all other children are safe, please come to the main office so that we can say 'hi' and know who is here!"

"All visitors *must* report to the office."

You can immediately feel what a difference the change in wording makes, with one encouraging people to say "hi" and the other reflecting a more punitive approach. While there are legal components to signage at schools and other service buildings, wording choices can be tailored to fit within those guidelines. What may seem like minor wording shifts can lead to big changes in engagement.

reflection

How might you work with families to establish a welcoming environment at building entrances and gathering space?

Explore the signage around the building. How might you shift wording on signs to make families feel invited while communicating a rule or policy?

Time and place

By putting extra thought and consideration into details when planning engagement activities, you can make families' experiences with your organization more positive. Anticipating the transportation and childcare needs of your families, and bringing events out into the community will help you reach more families.

Bringing programming out instead of people in

Going out into the community to employers and other organizations is one way to address access challenges for families, but is not the only way. Time and transportation frequently come up as common barriers to engagement. While these might seem like insurmountable challenges at times, there are some factors to consider that can help to reduce these stressors for families. Think about transportation resources that exist in your community to help people in being able to arrive to your building. Are you located near public transportation? If so, does your program start and end at times aligned with when the system stops near your building? Scheduling something to start twenty minutes before the bus arrives can deter many people who don't want to show up late, or who assume that missing part of the programming is unacceptable. Become familiar with the timing of the buses and trains, even if you do not take them, to avoid creating these challenges for families.

Consider timing with rush hour, or common nap times as well. If events or volunteering opportunities consistently fall within times of day that are challenging for families, you aren't likely see high participation.

Ask families how they arrive to your building, and what times of day work best for them to make meetings and events more accessible. Get creative about how you might extend your reach as well. Can families call into meetings? Is video conferencing an option to connect to people face-to-face? Do you need to offer the same event at two different times? Having multiple ways and times for families to participate in meetings and decision making, not just events, sends the message that you value their voice and the information they have to share.

Through Romero's experience, we've seen how establishing relationships with a large employer in the city can create spaces for engaging with families outside of the school. You may not have one large employer who would be your main focus for outreach, but are there other natural gathering places where families in the community have established trust and would serve as access points?

You might also consider what exactly you are going out into the community to do. Often organizations and schools bring events and activities out into the community, but you also can bring resources for or information about children out to families. For example, you might not only bring workshops or groups to the various outside locations, but also bring computers and set aside time for parents to ask questions about their children's grades, attendance, or development. Academic data can be intimidating, but providing ways to access the data in the comfort of their own neighborhoods can make it a little less so. Armed with this information, parents feel more knowledgeable when they go into the school to engage. They are empowered with knowledge about how to access this information in new ways as well, which they have learned in a place that is familiar to them.

Taking your programming or meetings on the road can say a lot to families. When you go to families it says, "I value your participation so much that I am willing to come to you to make that happen." Or, "I think this information is so important for you to access that I will come to you to make sure you can."

Why did Romero go outside the school in the first place? He knew that many of the families in his district were unfamiliar with the school system in the U.S., and didn't feel comfortable walking into the schools. Families in his district are not alone in their discomfort going into their children's schools or early childhood settings. In other districts, the reasons may be different: lack of experience, previous negative experiences, or negative feedback from other parents or staff. You may find that meeting families on their own turf first builds the trust that will later help them come to the building, now that they can find a familiar face.

Of course, one organizational partnership will not make everyone comfortable. The same applies to various neighborhoods: there may be certain social lines that families will not cross. Because of this you'll need to create multiple partnerships based on where various families will feel comfortable engaging.

Childcare

Aside from time and transportation, another barrier to engagement that we often hear from both families and the field is a lack of childcare. Parents may want to be engaged, but feel like their children aren't welcome to events, or that only one child is allowed if the event is related to the classroom. Providing childcare demonstrates to families that you want them there, and their whole family is welcome. However, childcare often requires funding and space, two things that you might not have access to.

One early childhood program demonstrated a creative way not only to keep kids entertained, but also to reduce parental distractions. During the parent meeting, they used long tablecloths to create a fort under the table that was full of blocks, books, and other things for kids to play with. Children were close by and occupied, not distracting to the parents who were trying to listen to information. A play area in a corner could have worked, too. The children in this example were old enough to play without constant supervision, so you may need to get more creative with active toddlers!

Babies can join, too, if you have the right attitude. Parents may be hesitant to show up with an infant, so make a point of encouraging moms and dads to bring their little ones with them. When the babies cry, squeak, or nurse, normalizing the behavior with a warm smile will make parents feel more at ease. When a toddler started babbling during a family gathering at a local non-profit, the facilitator seamlessly included the baby into the conversation, noting that the baby wanted her opinion heard too, which made everyone chuckle. This use of humor normalized the babbling and let the parent know it was all OK!

At any age, treating the children as part of the family, and thus part of the process—rather than a distraction—is what will feel most welcoming. Consider how you might engage parents and children in an activity together to process the information (if the topic allows). Some other places you might look to for low-cost or free childcare include:

- With supervision, scout troops or teens from the organization can help with the younger children.

- High school counselors may know of students who need volunteer hours.

- Partner with a community childcare or church who may have members or staff willing to donate time. You may offer to do the same for them.

Providing safe support for children during events or meetings will put families at ease. Families who feel comfortable are more likely to listen, speak up, ask questions, and gain access to the information you're sharing.

reflection

What community partners are already working with your organization that may be willing to provide a space for you to meet with families?

What kinds of activities or information sharing are you bringing to families in their community? What is one new community-based activity you would like to try?

In what ways are you offering childcare to increase opportunities for families to engage? How might you expand those opportunities?

Access to information

Schools and organizations are now gathering information on everything, from how the school functions to the data being collected about a child. Sharing this data, and how this data is used, strengthens partnerships with families by increasing trust and sharing the power of information. Families also need to know basic things like who to talk to when a specific problem arises, or how their child is doing during the day. Many organizations aren't used to being so transparent. It takes a shift not only in mind-set, but also in communication style, in order to effectively engage families with this information.

Home languages

For many families, interacting with education professionals can feel like they are talking to someone in a different language. And, of course, for some it quite literally is a different language. According to the National Center for Education Statistics, more than 4.4 million U.S. students are learning English at school as a second language, which can make communicating with home a real challenge at times.

Imagine being a parent who does not speak English, yet information from school or community organizations continues to be sent home with their child exclusively

Similar language, different meanings

Even people who speak the same language may have difficulty understanding each other. Cultural context and use of language can vary greatly across various regions, and even within neighborhoods that are only a few miles apart. Making information accessible in families' languages may also mean considering the tone and regional implications of certain phrases and words.

If you are unsure of how a phrase or tone might be understood, you may consider reaching out to families with whom you have built relationships, or staff within your building, who are familiar with possible perceptions and cultural interpretations for review.

in English. How would you respond to this information? Not only can you not understand the language, but you are also unable to access the information that is contained within those documents or messages.

In order to make information accessible to families, we must first know what language is primarily spoken in the home. As you consider how to gather information from families that can inform your interactions with them, you probably will want to ask what language they are most comfortable communicating in.

Some of us are working in incredibly diverse areas and may know or learn that there are hundreds of different languages or dialects being spoken at home by families. While you may not be able to provide translators for every language due to cost concerns, you may be able to find other ways to provide information in multiple languages. There are many low-cost translation services for written material online, but you may also consider tapping into your biggest resource— the families themselves. This might be a great opportunity for parents to be able to support the school or organization in a meaningful way by translating written material into their native language, or editing materials you have translated with an online service to ensure they make sense before they go out to other families.

This may also be an appropriate time for your agency to connect and partner with other organizations in the area who are serving the same community. Do some exploration to figure out who is providing translated materials in your area, and approach them about a potential partnership. You may also be able to share the cost of translation services if that would support families in multiple agencies.

You can also use these conversations as an opportunity for you to learn how a family's language addresses certain topics, or how the rules of their language may vary from English or other prevalent languages. Language is a great window into cultural norms, and knowing something about the usage can support you as you shape other messaging and materials.

Reading level

What's the reading level of your materials? Use the free "reading level check" on word processing programs to find out. You can find this setting under the Spelling and Grammar preferences on the review tab in Microsoft Word, and in similar places on other programs like Google Docs. A fifth-grade reading level or below ensures that most families will be able to understand the material. These free tools can be a great support for engagement with information, and can help you as you create written documents.

Jargon

Have you ever been at a workshop where you were unfamiliar with the topic and all you heard when people were talking were acronyms and technical terms for which you had no context? What context did you need? Did you take any information away from that experience? If you're anything like us, you probably found it difficult to follow or absorb much of anything that was being presented.

This experience can be all too familiar for families as they try to enter the world of their child's education. As we read in the chapter "Respect", words and phrases that are common to professionals can be confusing or have little meaning to families.

Often, when we talk about quality in early childhood settings, or education at any level, we use professional jargon and terms that resonate with our colleagues, such as:

- Developmental milestones
- Screening
- Scaffolding
- At grade level
- Performance assessments

While these terms may be familiar to staff, they may be part of a totally different language for families who are not surrounded by these terms daily. Making sure that families have the language they need to participate might mean that the organization alters their language, using less profession-specific jargon.

Part of engaging families successfully is supporting families in deepening their knowledge of the professional lingo, which includes providing definitions of this specialized jargon. For example, by sending home information that includes the words or vocabulary they may hear prior to a meeting, or having a professional development day for parents, you can empower them to become more active participants in conversations around data and outcomes. We must bridge the gap for families by providing them with the meaning behind those words.

from the field

"If I am a gatekeeper," explains Oklahoma City social worker Renea Butler-King, "it is incumbent upon me to help the client, or the person that I am working with, to understand what it is that I understand about the system. But it is equally as incumbent upon me to stretch myself to understand whatever the language is that they are bringing to the table, and the culture piece that they are bringing to the table, so that we can figure out how to get on the same page."

Butler-King flips the idea of gatekeeping on its head. "Our job as gatekeepers is not to keep people out, but to make sure that the flow is steady," she says, "and that everyone is getting through and not holding up others from getting through."

reflection

Consider the ways the information you are sharing with parents is presented. What platforms do you use to share information that are available across multiple languages or literacy levels?

How might you ensure that professional jargon is used appropriately, or that families have access to resources that support their understanding of the jargon?

Access to influence

We've saved the most difficult aspect of accessibility for last: who sits at the table where influence happens. It's clear that when families' voices are brought into decisions the process gets messier and takes longer—and the results are much more sustainable. We discussed joint or shared decision making in the chapter "Trust", but families are only able to be a part of the decision-making process if they first have access to a seat at the table—to the place where influence happens.

There are many ways that you can create opportunities for families to be in positions where they can have influence, both through their individual experiences and for the wider organization. Having family representation on various committees or holding focus groups to gather information from parents are ways that many organizations have found to be effective in inserting family voice into projects and plans. Having spaces for families to be a part of these conversations may lead to insights that we as professionals might not have thought about. Sometimes those insights save an initiative from flailing or failing, so your organization doesn't have to start over. Whatever the outcome, families voices are crucial for the true partnership you're hoping to build.

Having multiple seats at the table

Remember that allowing families to have access to places of influence does not simply mean having one seat in a room of many. It can be intimidating to be the only parent representative, and some people with valuable information to share might not be comfortable sharing in a room where they feel like an outsider. Consider having multiple family representatives in order to create an atmosphere that welcomes conversation from all parties, and does not make a parent representative feel like a token person in the room, or that they don't actually have any ability to influence.

Planning visits and curriculum decisions

What will children be learning about, and how is the organization planning to present that material? In many organizations this is a question that is answered in a completely internal fashion. What would it mean to open the door to families—to allow access to that process as equal partners? Access to influence within the organization means that, when these important discussions and debates occur, we have opened the organization up to families' insight and opinions. Instead of one-sided conversations, we have the option of forming a collaborative committee that includes

equal representation of families and staff members. Many schools are already creating groups that include parents and families in their programming, pedagogy, and curricula decisions.

While we might typically think of elementary schools and higher when we think of curricula, this collaborative approach to what children learn applies to home visiting and early care and education as well. Even if families are not influencing what curriculum is used, they can partner with home visitors and other staff to guide what information is presented, and when—for example, deciding what information is covered in the next visit, ensuring it is most relevant to them.

Having an attitude of "we're learning how to do this together" helps, because families aren't used to collaboration either. One person involved with a home visiting program offered that "it can take time for parents and caregivers to get used to the idea that they design and conduct the visits with our educators, rather than passively welcoming a 'teacher' for their child." In home visiting and other service delivery areas, it is critical that families are a part of planning the discussion topics because that information is designed to reinforce their parenting. Without input it is more challenging to get buy-in, and buy-in is where change occurs.

Advisory councils or committees

Advisory councils or committees are another way families can access shared power in your organization. You may have, or wish to have, an advisory committee that is made up entirely of parents, or that is a blend of parents, staff, and other community members. A blended committee is one way to gather input from various points of influence in the community, while at the same time gaining insight into how those opinions and needs influence each other.

Advisory councils can be a powerful tool, but only if implemented correctly. It is easy to ensure that an advisory council has parent representation, but it is harder to ensure they are being heard. Many have one or two seats for parents at the table, with several other folks in positions of influence from various organizations. These situations don't often create spaces where families are actually heard.

The facilitation and leadership of the group also plays a role in setting up a safe space to engage. One parent told of her experiences as part of an advisory committee at her child's preschool. She recalled one meeting that was framed as a conversation to gather potential input. In reality, however, she and other parents that were present were simply talked at. She noted several things that shifted the dynamic in the room, but the most important was the facilitation of the group. She stated that there was a skilled facilitator leading the discussion, but that person was interrupted by the principal, who was sitting in the room as well. The power dynamic, along with the less refined facilitation skills of the principal, shifted the meeting from the anticipated discussion into the "information session" she felt it became. Her advice to the schools? Be aware of power dynamics in the room, and focus more on who should be leading the meeting—not because of their status, but because of their facilitation skills.

We are not suggesting that organizations turn over all decisions to families. However, being open and honest with families about decisions creates buy-in at all levels. Even if you are not going to integrate all the feedback families give you, what you can do is explain the rationale for the decision that was made. Though families may still be upset, letting them know why a decision was made will demonstrate that you listened, and that you want them to continue to be involved.

Power dynamics

Access to influence is greatly influenced by power dynamics. According to author Cornelis Heijes, these power differences can be real or perceived, and they may be experienced differently by each involved party. It can be difficult to understand perceived power dynamics, especially if you have a position of power (most often anyone associated with the school or program has some level of perceived power to families). Think about the many ways that power dynamics can be made evident through daily interactions:

- **Titles or honorifics that are used when addressing people**—Are staff 'Mr.' or 'Mrs.'? Are parents also?

- **Who is leading/facilitating events or conversations**—Are staff always the "keepers of information" or are they at times leading next to parents as equals?

- **Seating arrangements**—Spreading out staff throughout the room can help to avoid an "us vs. them" dynamic where staff all sit together at the front or back of the room and seem unapproachable.

Leadership's presence, in any capacity, can impact the feel of a room. When administrators act as a participant, and not in their typical leadership role, it tangibly shifts the power dynamic. This might be an uncomfortable shift at first, for both the families and leadership who are sitting side by side with families. It may be difficult to surrender control in a space where one typically has it—as highlighted by the example of the principal who jumped into the role of facilitation when maybe she should have taken a back seat. It may be awkward for families to talk about more personal conversations with administrators or staff if they can feel a strong sense of the power dynamics playing out in the room.

However, these situations offer a tremendous opportunity for leadership to model vulnerability—to have real conversations as a participant, and as a parent, instead of as an administrator, teacher, or home visitor. These conversations offer staff a view into families' worlds they might not otherwise get, and vice versa. They can be the building blocks for empathy coming from both sides of the aisle. If you truly wish to get to know your families, it sometimes takes getting your feet on the ground and becoming a true part of the group.

Leaving titles at the door

Whether we like it or not, titles and roles come with power, perceived or real. These titles may be a barrier for families with whom you are trying to partner.

Creating a space that does not emphasize hierarchy, but rather one that creates a sense of teamwork and an even playing field, impacts families' sense of belonging. When you reduce titles' prominence and perceived importance you are likely to reach more families.

You might be wondering what this looks like in practice—how do you reduce the prominence of titles in your organization or school? As an example, let's take a moment to think about introductions.

Reflect on a scenario where a principal is attending a parent group. She will be a regular participant and not a leader. How might each introduction below impact the overall tone and engagement level with the group:

- "Hi everyone, my name is Mrs. Smith and I am the principal of this building, for those of you who might not know me. I am so glad to be able to join this group with all of you."

- "Hi everyone, I am Mrs. Smith. While some of you may know me in other roles, I am excited to be joining to sit and learn alongside each of you as a member of this group."

While both introductions are friendly, the second version (without the title) makes it clear that she is there as an equal member of the group. Small shifts in language can create open doors for families to really get their voices in the room, without worrying about whether they are "qualified" or have the power to speak out.

Titles and roles impact peer relationships among professionals as well. One parent educator described the difference it made in her work when she knew that leadership cared less about what their job titles were, and more about the work. "I felt more comfortable when the people in leadership positions were seen as servant leaders, as team players, as people who were not afraid to do any part of the work, and supported staff and parents in any way they needed. There was not a power-over structure but instead each team member had an important role and many skills and abilities to contribute to the overall well-being of the organization."

As your organization begins to offer more authentic ways for families to access influence, there are likely to be growing pains within the organization. Some staff members will naturally feel joy in seeing families engage. There are likely to be other staff members in your organization, perhaps those who have worked to achieve certain roles or leadership positions, that will have more resistance to providing families access to these types of roles. It can feel like a challenge to them personally, if they are used to being in a position of control, and can raise concerns about things being done the "right way". They may need support imagining another way.

A survey respondent shared an example of this kind of tension during one of the organization's first parent cafés. Parents participated in the planning of the event, and then acted as table hosts. The boost to the parents' confidence was visible. Afterwards, however, one of the other staff members "complained that one of the hosts [a parent], who had no previous similar experience, was a bit less than professional in her delivery and commentary." For the respondent, the families' leadership at the tables was a success, and she recognized that skill development was a part of the process. For some colleagues, the desire to control the outcome, or discomfort at not being able to manage the event, will overshadow the benefits.

It's important to acknowledge these feelings! Use supervision or other opportunities to talk about challenges or concerns staff are having around shared power and strategies they may use to address them. Explore with them how sharing power can lead to more genuine partnerships with parents, and does not mean they lose their role or expertise.

Power dynamics have a function, some good and some less than ideal. They are often ingrained within the environment, making them quite challenging to even notice, let alone to adjust. There are times when having a strong power dynamic is advantageous. However, there are many more times when a strong partnership is the more productive relationship structure. Have honest conversations in small groups or as a staff about the challenges of change, the goals of shifts in power, and how to work toward solutions that are both personal and interpersonal.

In what ways are families able to participate in decision making within your organization or school? What other opportunities can be explored?

Take a moment to reflect on your own feelings as you think about sharing power with families. What emotions are surfacing for you?

What avenues are there in your organization to address feelings of concern or unease that staff members might be experiencing?

Why it matters

Not all families will engage, regardless of the efforts that are put into making it easier for them to be able to. However, some families are not engaged simply because there is something—physical or emotional—blocking their ability to do so. While organizations cannot change a family's decision to engage or not, they can eliminate as many barriers as possible. Some of these barriers might be obvious. You might know that a family does not have access to transportation, for example. Others might be much more subtle, and you might not be aware of the fact that your organization is creating a barrier. You might also come across barriers to engagement that are not mentioned here—there are hundreds. Some of these might be unique to each family, while others might be more universal. Even if you cannot eliminate all the hurdles that families may come across, going out of your way to attempt to ease the many challenges that families face can speak volumes about your commitment to making sure they have the information they need, and that hearing their voice matters.

Accessibility

Extending an invitation is great, but it's important to consider accessibility. If everyone is ready, willing, and able to participate, they are more likely to accept the invitation.

moving forward

There are many aspects to accessibility. Take a moment to reflect on the previous chapter and think about which ideas, strategies, or pieces of accessibility are strongest, and which require growth.

> **Welcome**
> **Lightening and brightening**
> **Signage**
> **Bringing programming out instead of people in**
> **Childcare**

> **Home languages**
> **Jargon**
> **Planning visits and curriculum decisions**
> **Advisory councils or commitees**

We're strong on this:

We're so-so at this:

We're working on it:

Integration

The word "integration" carries many meanings. In *Aware: The Science and Practice of Presence*, educator and child psychiatrist Daniel Siegel defines integration as a process of, "allowing things to be different or distinct from each other on the one hand, and then connecting them to each other on the other."

This is the definition we are going to be operating from in this chapter: integration as a process that allows individuals to be themselves and maintain their differences, yet be able to find the links to other individuals in order to make a whole.

As we explore partnering with and engaging families, we are talking about bringing together all kinds of people—sometimes from very different places, and each with their own world views. These views and perspectives are what make individuals unique, and also what makes organizations and communities so strong. The challenge of integration lies in avoiding the tendency to try to make everyone fit the same mold, or imply they have to be in the system in the same way in order to belong. Siegel offers a useful analogy: integration is likened to a fruit salad rather than a smoothie. Each has a part in making the whole successful—without losing individual qualities!

Integration of various perspectives, cultures, backgrounds, and people can happen in so many ways. Sometimes integration happens at the individual level, while at other times it affects the whole organization. Sometimes we embody this value as we go about our work without even knowing it—it is naturally woven into our actions. At the organizational level, integration may happen naturally as well; this often depends on leadership having established a culture that values diversity in all forms: people, thoughts, and abilities. For many organizations however, it takes intentional planning and execution to build a culture in which the values that allow integration to flourish are fully embedded.

from the field

There are many times that we are not even aware of the multitude of social and cultural contexts that are represented around us. One parent educator shared that this is what surprised her most about doing home visits with families. "Seemingly similar families have such different views of programming and different needs," she commented, "and some families that appeared at first to be very different expressed similar needs."

Discovery

When you think about your organization, center, or school, what elements of diversity come to mind?

There may be families in the community that look very similar on the outside, yet have very different experiences at home. They may possess a belief system that aligns with eating a vegan diet, have a religious culture that is not often demonstrated in your school, or have any combination of other dimensions of diversity. Beginning to grow an awareness of the beliefs and experiences that exist within your community is an important place to begin.

Sometimes the process of discovery is as simple as asking. Families are often your best source of information. They are the experts on what makes them

from the field

In Redefining Parent Engagement: An Interview with Mary Jo Deck, *we are reminded that well-intentioned programs sometimes predetermine what they think parents need, rather than creating a way for parents to share their hopes, desires, wishes and concerns. To counter this, Shape NC, an obesity prevention program for young children in North Carolina, teamed up with the Buncombe Partnership for Children to use something called "photo voice methodology" to gain insight into families' lives—literally through their lens.*

The concept, as explained by Health Education and Behavior, *is simple: individuals photograph their day, and then share the photos they took. The pictures may be of objects in their home, daily life, or anything they experienced in a group setting over several weeks. Importantly, this methodology requires facilitated conversations about the photographs, letting the group see the world through the photographer's lens. In North Carolina, this project allowed staff to learn about families, to see the world through their eyes and in their own words. At the same time, it highlighted commonalities across families' and staff members' experiences.*

who they are. Be willing to learn, ask questions, be aware of indirect information, and be open to learning information that might contradict your assumptions or prove you wrong. It is important to remember that how we ask questions about individuals and their families matters. What is comfortable for each family to share and be asked about varies greatly. For the most part, when we ask questions as a genuine attempt to learn, it usually does not feel like an interrogation. In these conversations everyone may learn something new!

Though we do our best to be respectful of families, at times we may find out something new about families through mistakes, or actions perceived as mistakes. You might offer a family food during a time of fasting, or bring an activity to a home visit that uses food to a family that does not believe in playing with food. Making mistakes is fine, it is the response that follows missteps that can set the tone for future interactions. Recovering with grace, being willing to be wrong, and then using the information that you learned are ways to demonstrate to families that you want to learn and grow.

reflection

What social and cultural contexts exist within your own school or organization? How do you know?

What about in the larger community? How do you know?

How might you find out if your perceptions are accurate? Whom might you ask?

Making fruit salad

Over the years, the term "integration" has taken on a huge range of meanings; you've likely heard the word in the context of social justice (a means of addressing racial segregation); economics (a horizontal act of joining with competitors to create a monopoly); politics (countries uniting within a larger governing entity) and many other fields. The way we discuss the value of integration in this chapter does not refer to those contexts or definitions. We believe that family engagement work starts with intentional integration of families' cultures and social contexts—the

Differentiation

Differentiation is a worthwhile goal—but it's not feasible to use a different strategy to engage each person individually within your organization, due to the obvious capacity and time constraints. Identify multiple strategies that are the most successful with the greatest number of people, or with those whom you are targeting for a specific reason.

rich diversity of fruit in our salad—into the policies and daily work of schools and organizations.

Integration is not an easy task. It can be especially difficult when you are aware of the diversity that exists within the community, and are trying to ensure that all members are represented. You may have refugee or immigrant families from all different countries, mixed incomes, and diverse ages of parents and grandparents raising children. Each of these groups of people will respond to different engagement strategies in different ways, and each individual within those groups will have unique ways of responding as well.

The challenge of weaving in everyone's culture and individual needs can be daunting and overwhelming to staff. It is important to acknowledge the challenges and expectations you have of everyone, as well as the impossibility of being all things to all families. Remind staff that it's worth working through the challenges! When parents see themselves represented, even in small ways, they are more likely to feel welcome. When they feel welcome, families are more likely to continue to show up.

Social context and culture play a large role in whether families will choose to engage with you or not. You can help by discovering what engagement means to them, within their parameters, and then work within those. Engagement opportunities for families can be thought of in the same way we think of scaffolding learning. Structuring inviting and non-threatening opportunities can support families in building up their capacity to engage, as well as demonstrating to them that you value their input and participation. Gradually the supports can be removed as families' comfort, knowledge, and skills increase.

Socio-economic status and engagement

As we discussed in the chapter "Accessibility", what appears to be a disengaged family on the surface might in reality be a completely different story. For some families it might not be "normal" to engage in school, but that doesn't mean they aren't open to the idea. This may be addressed simply by exposure—no one has ever tried to engage them, or talked with them about why it is important. Regional differences and the type of communities people come from can have a large impact on their awareness of the value of engaging in their child's development and education as well. Conversations about the importance of engaging are more common in communities where there is access to more resources for education and support.

It is no secret that the socio-economic status of families impacts the experiences of children and families in education starting before they are born. This is also probably a big part of the reality of many of your daily lives as you work with families in your communities. Author Max Antony-Newman highlights research that has demonstrated that families from the middle class tend to be involved in a more hands-on way in their children's learning than working class families—often because they have more time and flexibility to do so. Families from under-resourced areas are more likely to adopt parenting approaches that emphasize children's abilities to make decisions independently, with less intervention from parents.

These differences are a result of a complex history between families and education systems, and if we look at the larger social context we can understand that the development of these differences are no fault of the families'. Schools and organizations that work with children have traditionally created more opportunities tailored to the way middle-class American families engage. Because of this, families that belong to other socio-economic groups are less likely to have opportunities to engage in ways that fit their needs and style. For example, many opportunities may occur during the school day at a time when salaried parents are more likely to be able to leave work for an hour. Events are also commonly scheduled without considering public transportation times. Opportunities that require parents to be present in the organization in order to participate also reflect the hands-on nature of engagement in middle-class families.

These differences can be especially obvious in organizations that serve families from diverse socio-economic groups. What might happen, even if it's unintentional, is that organizations offer opportunities to engage that only work for some of the families in the community, further highlighting the divide between the engagement levels of the wealthy and poor, as only more affluent parents are able to engage.

Though it can be challenging, and might reveal some uncomfortable truths about your organization, it is important to understand what might be impacting how families are able to engage, as well as if current practices are unknowingly driving a divide between families who have more wealth and those with less.

Socio-economic status and experiences with formal education systems are closely tied in the United States. Income often determines the schools and resources a person has access to, as well as their chances of completing formal education and moving on to higher learning. Statistically, those with lower incomes are more likely to have a lower level of formal education. Parents with low educational attainment may have had negative experiences with school, due either to the quality of school available to them, or other social implications. All of these factors influence the ways in which families will engage, and each requires unique strategies and support. It can be beneficial to all families in your community to expand the ways in which you offer parents opportunities to be active and involved—think of meaningful interactions that can occur both at home and in the building so families can choose what is comfortable for them.

reflection

How might some of your current engagement efforts or opportunities be making it challenging for some families to engage?

What are some opportunities you might offer to families who aren't accustomed to being asked to engage, to make them more comfortable?

When you extend that invitation, what might make them hesitate? What can you do to reduce their hesitation?

Offering multiple ways and times to make an impact in the organization is one way to begin to address these challenges, but it takes a systemic look to really shift patterns of engagement so that they include families of all economic levels.

Reflecting back on a strengths-based lens

As we touched on in the introduction to this book, despite best of intentions, sometimes those in "helping professions" can get caught up in a deficits mind-set. In doing so, families' strengths may be overlooked, as the focus is placed instead on the desire to help. Creating avenues for families to engage as partners means making room for everyone to use their strengths. This is the key to so much of this work. By embracing the values in this book and keeping the focus on families' strengths, you will come to see that there are so many ways to create paths for parents to come to the table—especially when we look at what families bring to us.

Identifying strengths

The characteristics that put families and children at risk have been well-defined and adopted by researchers and organizations for setting standards of service delivery (including Parents as Teachers, which uses the term "family stressors"). However, there is no widely used framework for identifying family strengths. Nevertheless, there is plenty of research that highlights characteristics that indicate family strengths. Some of the characteristics identified by the Search Institute include:

- Ability to adapt to change
- Community connections
- Caring for each other
- Commitment
- Humor
- Spiritual well-being
- Resilience
- Positive interactions
- Resourcefulness

The information you learn in overcoming challenges to integration will certainly be valuable to others, and many organizations are finding ways to share the strategies that they are using. Podcasts are one way to share stories and reach a variety of listeners. The Gente Puente ("bridge builders") podcast from the Hispanic Ministry Resource Center is one example that shares best practices for topics including family engagement, from Catholic religious communities across the United States. The podcast itself is bilingual—English sometimes and Spanish sometimes—depending on the language in which the guests are most comfortable expressing their ideas. The show's notes and summaries are available in both languages so that speakers of either language can still benefit from the content. Podcasts and other resources like these can help communities all across the country as they listen for strategies that can be adapted to integrate families in their community.

Identifying strengths can be difficult especially if you are unfamiliar with a family and their culture. However, it is important to take the time to explore strengths, especially when they don't seem obvious.

Strengths may not always look like what you expect them to. You may have to shift your perception of what strengths are when families' strengths don't match your current view. For instance, despite limited financial resources, a parent may be able to use household items to create developmentally stimulating play for their toddler. You may explore families' strengths through informal conversations or through formal assessments, whichever fits your current need. You may discover strengths in each other that were not obvious, yet when combined, create a powerful partnership. Integrating these strengths into services can create an easier path for families to engage, and programming that better reflects the community.

To clarify, it is not a bad thing to want to help families! It's likely that you chose the profession that you did because you enjoy helping people. Yet it is important to realize that, more often than not, families have the capacity to help themselves, and can actually help you help them in the most effective ways.

Bringing families' strengths to the forefront is beneficial in so many ways to the families themselves, but there are also countless ways families' strengths contribute to the growth and overall strength of your organization. No one knows their children and their community better than families, and the integration of this knowledge into the policies, practices, and curricula can only make them stronger for all of the children you are guiding and teaching.

Filling in gaps

As you are working with families and staff to build strengths, you might be identifying some gaps in knowledge that, if filled, would build capacity for engagement. By providing knowledge and experiences to fill those gaps, organizations are able to begin to level the playing field and give families and staff the tools that they need to engage. A 2015 study in *Teachers College Record* highlighted the importance of filling in gaps in knowledge by studying school choice policies. They found that, even when given the choice to change schools in order to improve their access to quality education, students were not reaching their full potential. They attributed this to a discovery that students were independently making the choice of which school to attend. Even when parents were involved in making the decision, it was based on a very limited set of information. Families needed support to fill in gaps about what they should have been looking for in schools, and to make sure that the school they were considering was not just a "quality" school, but a good fit for their student.

Policies such as this should take into careful consideration what information is available to families, and what might still be needed, in order to make them effective. Giving families choices in their child's education is great—but those choices need to be supported to ensure that families are given all of the information they need to make them. Policies are more likely to reach the intended outcomes when families are able to navigate their choices fully.

Families certainly may need resources that you have access to, or they may need you to share the knowledge that you have. How you share that information matters—and sharing it with the strength of the family in mind will help them process and apply the information, and may uncover a new strength. For example, when sharing information with parents about supporting their child's learning, connect the strategy to common practices in their community, or an interest or strength of the parent. A math skill can be practiced when visiting a food truck or waiting for a bus. A parent's ability to organize events in their family or community can be connected to the skills of sequencing. Pointing out what a family already knows and relating it to their child's learning increases families' confidence and ability to support their child. Maintaining a strengths-based perspective shapes the tone of the dynamic. It shows families that you aren't looking "down" at them or think they cannot do for themselves without your expertise. It lends families the dignity they deserve, and sets the framework for positive interactions.

Cultural Models

According to Marisa Gerstein Pineau, cultural models (also sometimes called implicit or unconscious biases) function as cognitive shortcuts that help you make sense of the world around you. Understanding how these shortcuts developed for you is important, because they may conflict with new information you're receiving in the journey of integration. If you know why you believed something in the first place, you can compare those old beliefs and examples with the new information. We all use cultural models. These models aren't inherently negative—even though you may discover that some of yours are inaccurate. You may find that when you learn and grow with families on a personal level, your cultural models are challenged or reinforced. These conversations with families are so important because they allow both staff and families to gather new information that helps to shape more accurate cultural models or ideas.

What does integration with families really look like?

As organizations become more intentional about integrating the social and cultural diversity of the families they work with, they might find that they get more creative about finding ways to involve and represent all members of the community. By infusing engagement opportunities with hospitality, and putting thought into the ways that families will see their own cultures represented, we can more fully integrate families into our organization.

Offering hospitality and exchanging information

When food is overly communicated as an incentive, it can end up decreasing the value families place on the event. However, offering hospitality is different than incentivizing, and offering and accepting meals is one way that culture is often shared. Providing opportunities for families to share their own food—whether old family recipes or specific cultural dishes—can create a welcoming and family-friendly tone for interactions at events.

The National Association for Family, School and Community Engagement noted that in settings designed to facilitate a give-and-take of information, food can be a shared experience that puts people at ease. Examples of this abound, from schools to city governments. In conversation with PATNC, one school administrator described how "Chat and Chew" discussions have become a cornerstone of her district's plan for gathering feedback from families. Another said that their "Slice of Advice" evenings—where participants contribute foods eaten by the slice, anything from pizza to pies—  incorporate both social interactions and a two-way flow of information directly related to a topic chosen by families. A city government official uses the Spanish concept of a *sobremesa*, or time for conversation after a meal, as an opportunity for constituents and political leaders to discuss challenging topics after they have gotten to know one another while eating together.

While food can be a great opportunity to build community, it may not be a fit for your community. Organizational policies and budget constraints, both individual and organizational, may make providing food a challenge. Be sure that by asking families to contribute food you are not stretching them into an uncomfortable space financially, or creating a divide between those who can and who cannot contribute. You may want to explore partnerships with local restaurants or markets that can provide ingredients for families to prepare food together! Taking individual financial investments completely out of the conversation eliminates the challenges that some families may have.

Integration vs. show-and-tell

Take a moment to reflect on the difference between highlighting a family's culture and integrating it within daily practices. Both are wonderful opportunities to recognize differences, but integration not only acknowledges differences, but also normalizes differences. While highlighting various cultures with "special events" or "nights" is important, if this is the only time you are integrating cultures, it can feel more like show-and-tell than an appreciation of a multitude of identities. Each of these examples demonstrates to families that not only do you want them to participate and be a part of your community, you also respect their culture and recognize them as an integral piece of the overall organization. Be intentional about representation where it matters, and you will observe an increase in the number of families who are willing to engage.

Representation goes a long way

Engagement increases when families see themselves represented in the engaged members of the community. This may not happen all at once. It takes time to build a community of engagement—and can take even longer to shift the demographics of an already established community. Use knowledge and input from families with whom you have built a connection to learn how to reach others in the community. You may not have a connection with a large number of families,

from the field

In one preschool classroom with a large population of immigrant and refugee families, staff found a way to reflect their community in the décor. While studying a unit on countries of the world, they hung up a large world map and placed markers to indicate where children in their classroom were from. One day, after the unit was over, but before they had taken down the map on the wall, a parent who was new to the school saw it and realized that there were other families from her country at the school.

The wall map supported parents in getting to know others from their country of origin, and it also provided a starting point for conversations that deepened connections between families and the staff. The staff decided to leave the map up as a way to support families' integration into the school community.

but that's OK! Each relationship you have matters, and each has the potential to grow into another. As you continue to build relationships and demonstrate that you value opinions and knowledge from all families, you will increase the number of families you are connecting with at a deeper level.

As we discussed in "Accessibility", you may wish to do a self-assessment of community representation in the physical space of your building. Small gestures that reflect families and the community make a big difference in families' comfort level walking into the building. For those families that are hesitant to come into the building because of a cultural norm, or previous experiences with similar organizations, it can be impactful to see someone familiar or something that speaks to them.

There are ways to use décor and furniture to help put families at ease when they walk in. In the cultures of your families, what items are common to have on the walls or on tables? You might ask families to bring in something that represents their family, or religious or cultural pieces, to share with the school. Using these items as permanent décor not only highlights the incredible variations that exist within your families, but also creates a sense of familiarity for those who may be new.

reflection

What types of opportunities for engagement can you offer that might demonstrate hospitality to families?

Explore the décor of your building. How does it currently reflect the community?

What strategies can you use to reflect families in your space, even when it looks very different from their homes or other community buildings?

What does integration look like in organizations?

As we put effort into shaping organizational practices with families, it's important to consider how policies that promote integration in a meaningful way are being developed as well.

Policies and practices

When we asked families on a PATNC family engagement survey what works and what doesn't when it comes to policies about engagement, what we heard was: "Family engagement doesn't happen when decisions are made without input from families. Planning and follow-up need to happen based on family needs and collaboration." This theme was repeated again and again. Policies and practices that guide conduct and processes in the organization are most effective when they are shaped within a community. For example, what if there is a rule against head coverings in the building, but you have families who practice a faith that requires a head covering? The rule might exist for a safety reason, but collaborative problem-solving discussions can help you find a way to balance safety and respect for the cultures of all families.

As our country grows and expands to embrace cultures from all over the world, there are some who are distressed that discussions of integration are taking place. Their definition of "integration" may be more like cultural assimilation—working towards a cultural uniformity rather than highlighting the unique differences that make a successful whole.

How to acknowledge and respond to these beliefs is useful to consider as policies and practices to foster integration are established. While integration of various people and ideas might seem new or scary for some, it can become a positive support if learning and exploration are structured well. This is why buy-in from individuals at the top of administration is critical; they are the ones who will stand up for the policies when frustrated individuals feel threatened by, or scared of, integration. Leadership can support staff by having clear guidance on how to engage in conversations to explore these challenges in a productive way by redirecting the conversation to policy and practice, or to connect it to the benefits for everyone, which can help the community grow together.

While most of us would like to live in a world where families and cultures are integrated seamlessly, reality is often very different than that. Having policies and protocols around things like harassment and discrimination within your organization may not stop them 100% of the time, but it does demonstrate to families that you value having a well-thought out response and plan for prevention and intervention.

Remember that staff might be the ones who are challenged by the thoughts of integration. Have honest conversations in supervision or other settings to address these challenges in open and productive ways. Simply telling staff what they "should" be doing won't always be an effective strategy, especially with a topic as sensitive as this.

While policies like these are critical, we also know that they alone cannot do all the work. Polices must be backed by action. Opportunities for training for staff, students, and the community can provide knowledge of all forms of diversity, but so can opportunities to simply get to know each other in comfortable spaces. Having built-in policies and protocols that ensure that these types of gatherings between families and staff happen, and are prioritized, can also provide time for staff to get to know what policies will best support families.

How might you explore diverse practices within your community in a way that supports those who are hesitant to change?

In what ways can you learn together, as a community, without highlighting a culture as "different," but rather as an integral piece of the whole?

Staff representation

As families look to find themselves represented in your organization, they will also look for staff members who remind them of themselves. If your staff does not reflect the community, consider that when hiring for the next open position within your organization. It is not realistic to have staff members that can reflect every variation within the community, of course, but being intentional about diversity in hiring practices can have a big impact.

Physical appearance is an obvious part of representation; it can play into those cultural models we described earlier in this chapter. However, it is not the only form of representation families look for when they interact with your organization. Importantly, integration often comes down to attitudes. Seeing families as partners is not a universal trait that all professionals bring to their work. When hiring, it can be difficult to know what biases individuals have; moreover, it is impossible to hire someone with zero biases. However, it is important to follow your intuition when red flags are presented. Asking questions during the hiring process about how an individual might work with a family in specific scenario can help you to identify whether potential candidates are looking at families through a strengths-based lens, or with other biases.

Integration policies and staff

   Conversations around integration often focus on the people who are engaging for the first time. Equally important are those who are already part of the community and feel safe there. If you reflect on the initial analogy we borrowed for integration—fruit salad—it's easy to visualize each piece being instrumental in making the whole. However, as you begin to grow and shape your "new" community, it might feel to some people as if they are being marginalized or getting squashed out of the whole.

   Staff are one group of individuals who will be a part of a potentially major shift. While some individuals will choose to leave if they do not like the direction the organization is going, others may stay but feel they are losing standing as the organization shifts toward giving families more input. We can't emphasize the importance of staff buy-in enough.

   It is important to acknowledge staff fears as valid, and support them in finding their role in the community. Ensure that efforts are made to incorporate staff culture as well, and that staff are a part of all conversations that engage the whole community. Individual conversations with staff can also remind them that they are all a part of the whole, and integrating their voices is also critical.

reflection

Are there staff members who look like the community within your organization? If yes, are they in support roles or leadership roles? Why might this matter?

How might you find out about individuals within the community who might be ready to be a part of your team when you go into a formal hiring process?

Blazing a trail together

On the journey toward engagement, we are asking families to go with us to a shared destination. It's not about us sending them forward, or us leading the way and having them follow behind on a path we have paved.

This idea of "paving the way" for families and children is probably familiar to you. It is how many organizations operate. Families can have good outcomes this way, and there are times when a challenge or a roadblock may necessitate our pushing ahead and clearing the way for families. However, this mentality may lead us to assume that the roadblocks for families are caused by someone else, when in fact sometimes they are made by organizations themselves.

Creating this path together allows families to get what they really need, not just what we think they might need, or how they need it. It also can be helpful to sit down and take a hard look at what it takes to access services or interact with your organization. While we all have competing requirements from funders or regulatory agencies, it is equally important to take the lens of a family, and see what they see. Are there requirements asking them to give more information than they are comfortable with, even if they desperately need the services? How many people do they have to interact with before they reach the person who can help them?

Author Brené Brown reminds us that researchers can measure the impact of collective assembly—situations where people feel connection and communal emotion. They've found that they contribute to a sense of meaning in life, a positive outlook, social connectedness and decreased loneliness.

"I feel that we strive to meet families where they are, figuratively and literally. We are home visitors, so we are in families' comfort zones. They have invited us into their personal space. We come prepared with materials or information that families have asked for. I feel it is really self-directed for the families we serve. There is an element of psychoeducational work with each family, but they are also choosing the trajectory of where we go, and we, as support workers, are there to be co-explorers with the families on their journey. We don't just lead the way—a true partnership could never work like that."

– 2018 PATNC family engagement survey

Bringing it all together

Integration is not simply making room for someone by moving someone else out. It's about growing together into a new community that works for everyone. Dual-learning opportunities, like the ones mentioned in the chapter, "Respect", are one way to pull everyone along together and support awareness of how to engage with each other. The change can be challenging, but the more opportunities you provide to learn and grow together, the smoother the journey will be.

What we are trying to do is to create a space where everyone—staff, families, and members of the community—feels comfortable engaging at a level that's right for them, in a way that works towards an end goal of true, honest partnership.

This goal really means to create a space where everyone gets to choose whether to engage or not. They are not distanced because they don't feel like they belong. They are able to find a place for their voice and family to be heard. In her book *Braving the Wilderness: The Quest for True Belonging and The Courage to Stand Alone*, social scientist Brené Brown writes that in order to experience true belonging, "[w]e're going to need to intentionally be with people who are different from us. We're going to have to sign up, join, take a seat at the table. We're going to have to learn how to listen, have hard conversations, look for joy, share pain and be more curious than defensive, all while seeking moments of togetherness."

Integration of various perspectives, cultures, families, and individuals is challenging, but so very worth it. It also is not a task that will happen overnight, or have a continuous path forward. More often than not you might find your organization sliding backwards, or feeling like it's struggling to find what the "whole" even looks like. This is all normal! Each time a new individual or new family comes into the community it will take a few more turns. Each time a member of the community leaves, it will leave a gap that requires some shifting.

Each of these twists and turns will pull your community a little bit closer to its whole, the fruit salad that makes it so incredible. Like many of the things we discuss in this book, the work to integrate families and communities is never done—there is no finish line. However, it is critical work that will lay the foundation for deeper interactions with families, and positive outcomes for their children.

Integration

Within collective action, a deep level of commitment is required to acknowledge and utilize each individual child and adult, and recognize their contribution to the whole.

moving forward

There are many aspects to integration. Take a moment to reflect on the previous chapter and think about which ideas, strategies, or pieces of integration are strongest, and which require growth.

> **Socio-economic status and engagement**
> **Offering hospitality and exchanging information**

> **Representation goes a long way**
> **Policies and practices**
> **Staff representation**
> **Integration policies and staff**

We're strong on this:

We're so-so at this:

We're working on it:

Compassion

It is wonderful when someone sits with us and truly listens to us. It is powerful when we can see that a person understands our words and the emotions behind our words, which can be so difficult to convey at times. Not only do these conversations make us feel better, they can help us to move into action that alleviates whatever dilemma we may be facing.

Compassionate conversations, whether in our personal lives or professional lives, provide a space for gaining understanding and offering support. Compassion has long been associated with certain professions, usually those that are seen as "helping". No matter the profession, approaching individuals with empathy and compassion provides space for growth and change to occur within the context of deeper relationships.

According to a 2013 article in *Scientific American*, humans are hardwired to empathize; to truly connect with others is a basic human need. As we have been exploring throughout this book, the logistics and details of engaging families are nothing if we do not interact at the human level—with all of its messiness, beauty, challenges, and rewards.

Compassion: sympathetic consciousness of others' distress together with a desire to alleviate it.

– Merriam-Webster Dictionary

Each of you reading this book understands the human aspect of this work and how intricately it is tied to the outcomes that we hope to reach. You understand that the need for compassion and empathy is high. You also likely understand how challenging it can be at times to live these principles when all of the work that needs to be done is piling up.

We also recognize, and have experienced, that working with families day in and day out does not mean that you have good relationships with, or even like, all of them. It is hard work to be compassionate with those with whom you have already established good relationships, and even harder when you have to push through other feelings first. Adding to the challenge is that those who often require the most empathy and compassion of us are not always the easiest to give it to. Remember to give yourself a break, permission to lean out when needed, and the strength to lean in when you need to.

Sympathy, empathy and compassion: what's the difference?

For some, compassion comes naturally. These individuals might have a beautiful natural capacity, not only to listen and understand, but to

What does it really look like?

A parent is experiencing stress related to a concern they have about their child's delay in speech. Look to the reactions below to explore the differences between sympathy, empathy, and compassion.

Sympathy: "Having a child with a speech delay sounds like a difficult challenge."

Empathy: "I can see that you are really unsure of what the process looks like after this delay has been identified. I understand and relate to that feeling of being unsure or scared."

Compassion: "I can tell that you are really worried about your child continuing to have a delay. Why don't we sit down and explore some activities that you might choose do at home to support speech development while you wait to see a speech pathologist?"

seamlessly drift into solution-driven action while keeping a person-centered lens. For most of us, getting to a place where compassion flows naturally is hard work. We may have to fight our natural tendencies to steer away from "getting involved" in others' emotional journeys. We may think that we are expressing compassion, and then upon further investigation realize we were just skimming the surface of sympathy, or empathy.

Sympathy, empathy, and compassion are words we use fairly often, and interchangeably, to describe the ways in which a person interacts with or feels toward another. But these words are not actually interchangeable—they have different meanings and different outcomes when applied to relationships. There has been a trend in recent years to move from expressing sympathy for families to attempting to find deeper connection through empathy and compassion.

When sympathy is present, one individual acknowledges the feelings of another, but does not identify with those feelings or the individual circumstance. While not typically considered a negative emotion, sympathy, when misplaced, can come across as pity. This can leave the person who is sharing a difficulty to feel as though they are still alone, with someone who is looking in from the outside on their situation.

Empathy takes sympathy a bit further, past simply acknowledging a feeling, to making a personal connection to the feelings of the speaker. When we empathize with someone, we put ourselves in their situation, and communicate that we understand what they are going through. Empathy is when you truly "get" it—you feel what the other feels in a way that allows you to connect on a personal level, by imagining or getting in touch with how you might feel, or have felt, in that situation.

Empathy can be described as a stepping stone toward compassion. Compassion continues to build on empathy, pushing past the understanding of emotions, into a desire to act. Someone demonstrating compassion says, "I understand what you are feeling. I want to help you, how do we solve this problem that is in front of us?". It is when an individual understands the feelings of the listener (empathy), and connects that with a desire to alleviate the stress *through action*.

Compassion and the brain

When neuroscientists compared how our brains react to empathy and compassion, they discovered some fascinating differences. As noted by author Tara Well in *Psychology Today*, studies showed that when people completed an empathy training, the parts of their brains linked to emotion and self-awareness were active. However, when they completed a training in compassion, the parts of their brains linked to rewards and decision-making were most active. When tasked after the trainings, those who were trained in compassion were more likely to follow their emotions with actions than those trained in empathy.

Think about a time in the past when you were asked to listen to someone who was facing a challenge. Would you describe your response as sympathetic, empathetic, or compassionate? Why?

Reflect on a time in the past when you were faced with a challenge. What types of responses did you receive from listeners? Which did you prefer?

The how and why of the work

Compassion is essential because families are more likely to get, and stay, engaged when they feel cared for by staff, and can see it in their actions. In addition, compassion breeds compassion. People who experience compassion are more likely to be compassionate back, whether they are staff or families. This culture of compassion can go a long way in creating a space where families and staff feel supported, which fosters the strong relationships that increase engagement.

"The competent aspect of social work is crucial; we are worthless if we are incompetent. The compassionate aspect of social work is crucial as well; without compassion, we are just automaton/robots going through the motions of our day."

– Marian L. Swindell, "Compassionate Competence: A New Model for Social Work Practice"

Learning and growing

Being compassionate is hard work. Many of us struggle to be compassionate in a sustainable way. There is an innate vulnerability in being compassionate—you must be willing to have open and honest conversations with people that you might not know all that well. You must be patient enough to let others be vulnerable with you as well, and truly listen and support them in finding a path forward that works for them, not just what resonates with you as a quick fix.

There are many barriers to embracing and enacting compassion, both around us and within us. While it might seem difficult at times, compassion is not something that you either have or you don't. It may come naturally to some, but like many things, there are ways to teach compassion for the many of us who have to work a little harder to integrate it into our daily work.

A study published by *Psychological Science* demonstrated that increasing compassion is not only possible, but can be done over a relatively short period of time. This study explored the use of a compassion training intervention that took just 30 minutes a day for two weeks. After the intervention, participants demonstrated higher rates of compassion in a simulated scenario focused on helping others than those who had taken a different form of thought training for the same amount of time.

While most organizations don't have the time or resources to do a formal training intervention like this one, they can choose to use strategies to enhance compassion. There is a plethora of informal activities you can build into professional development or engagement events that cultivate compassion. Setting up opportunities for individuals to deepen relationships, no matter where they are starting, will build a foundation where compassion is more likely to develop.

Distress: what do we know?

Distress isn't always a shared experience, and sometimes it can be difficult to understand someone else's pain or specific life circumstances, especially if we have never been there ourselves. It can be tempting in these moments to jump in and say, "I understand", even when we really don't. While this can seem well-intentioned, it can backfire if it is clear to the individual you really don't understand.

Don't be afraid to pause and take a step back to let the family know you would like to understand, but need more information before you can work together towards determining an action plan. These moments of asking for clarification may feel uncomfortable at first, but can lead to genuine moments of compassion.

Getting personal

Compassion comes more naturally to us when we know each other. Through panel discussions we've learned of organizations around the country that are creating ways for families to connect and learn about each other in order to deepen relationships.

In the District of Columbia, the school chancellor meets families in their homes for "living room chats"—a more personal way to get to know the families than at the parent advisory cabinet or monthly public forums. Such visits give the leader of the school time to focus on families' hopes and dreams for their children (rather than being utilized as a promotional opportunity for the district or pushing an agenda). Families appreciate the time that is taken to get to know them as a family, and they also get to know the chancellor in a more intimate setting.

Other districts empower families to organize face-to-face, small-group conversations around topics that are important to them. In Portland, Maine, the Shared Space Café model builds bridges between the community and school by encouraging parents to lead intentional dialogues. In these conversations, all parties are provided with the topic in advance so they can organize their thoughts, making the conversations less reactionary and more reflective. Teachers and staff attend Shared Space Café sessions where they learn about topics that are personal to families—knowledge that deepens their understanding of what matters to families, and how they view the world.

Having knowledge of the hopes and dreams families have for their children can build stronger relationships between families and staff, and opens windows into why families do what they do. Knowledge like this can shape compassionate responses.

The Greater Good Science Center at UC Berkeley suggests some things to think about as we work to deepen our compassionate practices include to:

- **Look for similarities.** Finding ways that connect you to others can increase feelings of compassion; we want to help others with whom we feel closer.

- **Try to avoid blaming others.** When we focus on what others have done wrong, it reduces feelings of compassion.

- **Look at people as individuals.** This forces us to think about each person and his or her characteristics, rather than the stereotypes of a larger group they might belong to. When we take the time to get to know people for who they are, it makes it hard to not be compassionate when the need arises.

- **Work cooperatively.** Cultivating a sense of community and highlighting shared outcomes can support professionals and families in working together closely for the same end goal. In the process, they can get to know one other and look to each other as teammates instead of competitors.

These types of practices can be easily incorporated into inclusion activities, games, and team-building strategies during any staff development or engagement event. Some in the organization may wonder why so much time is being dedicated to cultivating compassion in this way. Research noted by Tara Well on brain development demonstrates the visible impact of compassion on the brain and behavior. These differences in brain activity after experiencing compassion impact how a person acts towards others. If we can change the way our own brains work by actively implementing compassion in our lives, we can impact the many people with whom we interact.

The better that staff and families get to know one another, the more likely they are to support each other in compassionate ways as they begin to feel that each of these relationships are worth the time and effort it might take to move through empathy and into compassion.

Compassionate care

Today, compassion is being widely implemented as more than just something that sounds good, but rather as an integral part of growth within an organization. Research that supports policies and practices that encourage compassion spans professions. It also bridges gaps to provide the best services to families.

In recent years, the healthcare field in particular has presented arguments and evidence to show that compassion is not just a nicety, but a necessity for quality care. Several studies highlighted by author and ethicist Marianna Fotaki state that compassionate care not only feels better to patients, but leads to speedier recoveries as care becomes more person-centered. The studies showed that doctors are more likely to be creative and relaxed when they experience compassion as well, leading to more innovative and personalized care. All of this leads to better outcomes for patients.

We can take these lessons from healthcare and apply them across a wide spectrum of service delivery. The business world, social work, and numerous other fields are already using these findings to push forward what it means to have quality work across the board. It makes sense that when we not only understand challenges, but actively work towards targeting solution-focused action, we have better outcomes.

from the field

Parent Map notes that through the work of the Campaign for Compassionate Cities, local governments and schools around the world are being recognized for their work to bring compassion to their communities. The Charter for Compassion says that those who demonstrate this value are impelled "to work tirelessly to alleviate the suffering of our fellow creatures, to dethrone [them]selves from the centre of our world and put another there, and to honour the inviolable sanctity of every single human being, treating everybody, without exception, with absolute justice, equity and respect."

Being awarded the label of "compassionate school" or "compassionate city" shows that these entities emphasize the importance of using compassion as a tool for overcoming barriers and fostering interdependence. They are setting examples for organizations and cities about how to build an environment where compassion is prioritized, and people excel together as a result.

How might you integrate activities that build habits of compassion into professional development or engagement activities?

What impact have you seen or experienced when compassionate care is present?

Challenges and hurdles to compassion

We have laid out some of the rationale for compassion, and a few of the barriers, but we know that if it were really that easy we would be acting with compassion consistently and effortlessly. We would venture to guess that no one reading this book is ever intentionally avoiding compassion. We also know that whether we are aware of it or not, sometimes it falls to the wayside due to internal or external influences.

Taking the time

Perhaps the biggest challenge to compassion flourishing within an organization is the relentless pace of busyness. Compassion takes patience and time. It means setting aside the minutes or hours needed to truly get to know a family, and then working through possible solutions. As we have mentioned in the previous chapters, relationships are built on trust, respect, and other key values—each of which takes time to develop. Families are unlikely to disclose struggles or challenges unless relationships include a sense of understanding and acceptance first.

Most of us can relate to the challenge of running out of time during the workday. It can feel overwhelming to take an hour to sit and talk with the parent who walks through your door unexpectedly. We can also probably relate to avoiding saying hello to someone, simply because we don't feel like we have the time to get into a conversation. However, these conversations, no matter how short, are the places where staff and families begin to see each other as individuals—that critical element of feeling compassion.

Whose work is this, anyway? Clarifying expectations

Perhaps it is tempting to think, *these parents aren't doing what they should do to raise their child, and it's making more work for me.* You may be right. Their life circumstances may be making more work for you. But in the long run, what are the outcomes you're trying to achieve? Many of us went into our careers with the express intent of building helping relationships, but this goal can easily get lost along the way as we begin to burn out. What if you looked at this parent as a teammate, someone with whom you share the goal of supporting this child in being successful? Odds are you will have better luck if you and the family work together, as partners, to find a solution.

It is very difficult to blame a family for their child showing up with poor hygiene every day when you learn that they have lost their home recently, and don't have stable housing. You probably won't scold the child who falls asleep in class when you discover that both parents work nights, which means the child is frequently up late at night caring for a baby sibling. You might support the family in the first example by providing a new uniform or offering access to the school's washing machine. You might support the family in the second example by providing a time or place during the day for the sleepy student to take a power nap so he can focus better in school.

Making these offers may not be the very first thing you do—especially if you don't yet have a relationship with the family. Pause, even if doing so takes you out of your comfort zone. Allow space for the family to take control of the pace and the options. One parent educator in a home visiting program in rural Missouri described the experience this way: "I can feel helpless at times because I can see and identify a need that a family may have, but they may not be ready to talk to me about it, because we need to spend time building a relationship. As a solution-focused person, it's important for me to step back and let the relationship form naturally. As workers, we need to reassure ourselves that families have been getting by for a long time without [our services], hang our 'hero' capes up, sit back and let the relationship progress naturally—then work with the family as the comfort level rises." These partnerships, where trust and respect grow, are often open to change down the road.

Acting with compassion and supporting families to find solutions does not mean over-functioning either. At times, it may be beneficial to be the first person to reach out, or do laundry for a family, to help them balance their own time and needs. We do this within the context of a partnership—not because we have decided what needs to be done. Reflect back on our conversations about building trust and growing partnerships. Telling families how to "fix" their problems or sending a message that you don't think they can do it themselves is not going to support the development of relationships. Finding a solution to relieve distress as a team, driven by the family, is compassionate support.

Solving problems with a family as a team also has the extra benefit of allowing you to get to see this family's strengths highlighted. Pay attention to resources they have—both internal and external—and support them in using those to come to their own solutions rather than pushing yours. Highlighting to families how their own strengths can solve a problem they didn't feel they were capable of solving? That is compassionate care.

Self-compassion

Just as we can learn to be compassionate towards others, we can learn to extend compassion to ourselves as well. In a *New York Times* article by Kristin Wong, Kristen Neff, a leading researcher on self-compassion, describes it as "treating yourself with the same kindness, care, and concern you show a loved one."

According to Neff, self-compassion teaches individuals to look at themselves more realistically and rationally. It can lead to stronger relationships as people acknowledge their own flaws and see themselves as human.

Social service agencies, especially those working with families every day, often tout the importance of self-care. Understanding emotions, listening without judgement, and finding solutions are all great skills to practice on yourself!

There are many resources available for those who wish to engage in a practice that supports the development of self-compassion. Just as compassion for others can be learned, so too can compassion for ourselves.

When we use self-compassion as a strategy, we give ourselves the gifts of patience and kindness, which helps us show the same to others.

Partnering vs. "helping"

In professions focused on providing support, it is easy to fall into a pattern of well-intentioned "helping" or "guiding" that is not actually partnering. These actions, though well-intentioned, can come across as ways that simply solidify the power differential between families and staff. It can appear that staff have the means and abilities to solve problems, and families do not. Doing for, and not with families, makes it clear that the actions are coming from sympathy, or pity—not from a strengths-based lens.

Authentic relationships are only possible when we see families as capable of dictating the terms of the partnership. This means we:

- Communicate with individuals as equals when talking about things related to their family. Better yet, we treat parents as the experts in situations that involve their child.

- Explore professional knowledge together with the family, and see how those ideas may be meshed with what they already know about their child and family.

"We have to get really real with ourselves and figure out how we can be authentic, so that we can allow the people who we are serving to become the same way—because the only way for us to help a family engage is if they let us. But if I've already made some decisions about them, how they should engage with me, then I am not giving them permission to come with what they have to offer."

– Renea Butler-King, social worker

reflection

How do you balance the demands of work and the time required to act with compassion?

Think of an example of when "helping" may have gotten in the way of partnering? How could the outcome have been different?

Developing a culture of compassion

Much of our conversation in this chapter has been focused on how individuals themselves can grow in their compassionate care. However, professionals are only able to do this if they are surrounded by organizations that not only understand the importance of taking the time to act with compassion, but allow the time and resources to make it happen.

Looking in the mirror

What does compassion in an organization look like? When researchers asked participants what it means to have a compassionate workplace, they answered that it meant they could talk openly with others at work about their problems and gather support without judgement. They also identified it as a place where they could not only ask for support, but actively connect with resources to solve their problems as well.

This study went on to demonstrate the link between a compassionate workplace and lowered stress levels, which leads to better employee outcomes. In other words, if employees feel compassion, they are more likely to be able to do their jobs well, and less likely to experience emotional burnout. If they are not experiencing burnout, they have more energy to dedicate to acting compassionately towards the families they serve.

Providing staff with opportunities not only to see but to demonstrate compassion in the workplace creates a window for families to see how they will be treated as well. If they can see that taking the time to be compassionate is prioritized between staff members, they can be assured that they will be given the time they need as well.

Promoting compassion

Ethicist Fotaki argues that, in order for compassionate care to truly occur, organizations cannot rely on individual practitioners' abilities to be compassionate in overcoming barriers created by policy. She states that policies and practices can both support and hinder compassion within the workplace. Just as compassion can be learned, it also can be suppressed by policies and practices.

Although it can be taught over a short period of time if there is a dedicated intervention, developing or strengthening compassion still takes practice and persistence. In most cases, compassionate responses may not be the quickest or most cost-effective way to address a problem either. This means that policies that support compassion and compassionate relationships must be flexible, and allow time for feelings to be heard and solutions or actions to be identified.

Organizations also are responsible for providing resources that allow staff to be confident in taking compassionate action. It can feel unpleasant when you can listen to someone, but cannot find any resources to support a compassionate action. When staff experience this, or know that they might, they may be more likely to express sympathy or empathy, but not support the family in moving towards action.

It is important to note that no matter the resources provided, an organization cannot enforce compassion in volunteers or employees—there is an element of individual choice. However, educational leaders emphasize that it is possible to include interview prompts that address compassion when hiring. For example, you might present a potential candidate with the following scenario: A parent is consistently missing their scheduled home visit because of a conflict in scheduling with the local food pantry hours. The only other time that works for the family is outside of the typical work hours of the home visitor. How would the parent educator respond to this? You probably would want to hear that the individual would sit and listen to the family, and then brainstorm solutions that would allow them to attend both.

reflection

Which official polices and official practices support employees in developing and demonstrating compassion? Which hinder it?

What does a compassionate workplace look and feel like to you?

Policies that emphasize the importance of taking the time to support families effectively, provide access to resources, and demonstrate a culture where compassion is key, all provide an environment that breeds compassion. Setting effective patterns for practice and establishing values that include compassion can guide everyone to think about compassion as a tool and a framework, rather than an afterthought or an outside force.

Compassion

Compassion is easy to recognize when we experience it—through large or small examples of empathy, emotional connection, equitable treatment, perspective taking, or simply a warm welcome to a new situation.

moving forward

There are many aspects to compassion. Take a moment to reflect on the previous chapter and think about which ideas, strategies, or pieces of compassion are strongest, and which require growth.

> **Learning and growing**
> **Compassionate care**
> **Taking the time**
> **Whose work is this, anyway? Clarifying expectations**

> **Partnering vs. "helping"**
> **Looking in the mirror**
> **Promoting compassion**

We're strong on this:

We're so-so at this:

We're working on it:

Initiative

The big picture of engaging families sounds nice, but in practice it can be difficult and overwhelming to get off the ground. For many of us it is uncharted territory, and we make the path as we walk it. As we prepare for change, we must ask some challenging questions and dig into work that continues to push us beyond the familiar.

The word initiative comes from the Latin *initiatus* or *initiare* (to begin), from *initium* (a beginning). Beyond the idea of taking the lead, initiative is also associated with words like resourcefulness and capability. In the context of family engagement, initiative holds both of these meanings— the ability to lay the foundation for engagement, as well as the ability to reassess, return to the drawing board, and respond creatively to challenges as you continue on the path of engagement.

Why do you want to do the work of engaging families? What meaning does it hold for you? The answers to these questions—our personal reasons why—are our motivation to do the work. Each individual walking with you on this journey has their own reasons, their own answers that drive them to move the needle of family engagement forward.

Whether you are just beginning family engagement initiatives on a broad scale, diving into a new project that is one small aspect of a larger vision, or getting to know a new family for the first time, initiative is part of the drive that gets you moving forward. Getting to know personal motivations, understanding the needs of the community, and setting targets and goals allow you to get creative in designing what family engagement will look like in your community. It takes a lot of work to get something going, but it also is a time to get creative and dig into real, messy change.

In this chapter and the next we will explore two closely related values— initiative and persistence. Digging into the work is hard, and struggling to keep going in the face of challenges often requires one to return, repeatedly, to the skills that support initiative.

Laying a foundation

Laying a foundation for family engagement requires planning and preparation. The most important work we can do when beginning to formulate plans and ideas is to consistently return to considering the needs of our partners in engagement, and think carefully about what we hope to achieve together.

Step one: identifying needs

Communities and individual families have such varied needs. Despite our biggest hopes and our best efforts, it is likely we will not be able to accomplish everything we set out to do. Identifying where to start can be one of the hardest parts about addressing a topic as daunting as family engagement—there are so many interrelated needs!

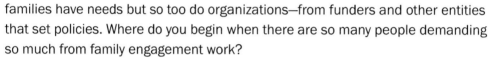

First, before you dive in, pause and let yourself know that you will not, and cannot solve everything—and that is perfectly OK. There are competing priorities that might feel overwhelming; families have needs but so too do organizations—from funders and other entities that set policies. Where do you begin when there are so many people demanding so much from family engagement work?

It can be tempting to dive headfirst into the first idea you have, or try to solve the first problem that comes your way with each new family you talk to, but it can be helpful instead to take a step back and attempt to look at the bigger picture. You never know what needs may be overlapping that can be addressed with a simple shift in an existing strategy, or which families may benefit from the same event or connection.

Using many of the strategies that we have addressed throughout this book— from surveys and interviews to focus groups or parent chats—organizations can establish partnerships with families that identify real, relevant needs of the community from the beginning of a plan or project.

This data-gathering phase of the work is critical; when we see ideas floundering it is often because they don't address real needs in the community. Group connections are planned without any input of the families who are expected to attend, and then no one shows up because the topic didn't resonate with them. Families come to a meeting anticipating having a voice in an issue they care about, but are provided with a steady stream of information instead, and given no time to provide input.

It can be easier if you are just beginning to talk with the families with whom you've established relationships. The odds of being successful in addressing families' needs increases when you know families more deeply.

This is not to say that gathering data around needs is impossible with families or areas of the community that you don't know as well. Going out into the community and beginning to build relationships demonstrates that you are invested in doing what the community needs, and will begin to give you a glimpse into the honest needs of families.

You might have tried to complete some form of a needs assessment with families, perhaps multiple times. You might have had a very low response rate—a frustration that is common with many organizations and schools. Or there was a high response rate, but the needs seem varied and vague. Maybe the needs are so numerous that they feel impossible to even begin to address. If these situations have happened to you, you are not alone.

It can be difficult to identify needs accurately if no one is very clear on what they are. This can happen in places where there are immense needs and it is difficult to sort out which are more important than others. It can also happen when there are relatively few obvious needs but rather subtle factors that, if addressed, could shift patterns of engagement.

Even though it can feel daunting, all of the data you have gathered around needs are important, and helps tell the story of the community and the families you serve. Look at the broad, big needs and attempt to narrow in on a few specific things that you know you can address. Are parents concerned about their children's kindergarten readiness? Maybe the best place to start is by focusing on supporting literacy or math development in the preschool years through events and engagement activities.

You can prioritize individual family, or organizational needs as well. By focusing on small, incremental points of impact that contribute to the greater concerns of the community, you will shape a great place to begin to dive more deeply.

It can be uncomfortable to ask families to open up about their needs, especially when it feels like the organization can't feasibly address them. Remember that just figuring out what needs are does not mean that you promise to "fix" any of them. What you can do, however, is to provide connections for families that demonstrate how the work comes together.

Balancing organizational needs

It can be difficult to balance the most pressing needs of the community and those identified by the organization. Funders have demands and requirements of schools and non-profits—and family engagement initiatives are often asked to address them. While it is ideal to assess needs of families, these organizational needs must also be met. You will have the best chances of success in these measures when they are tied to needs identified by the community.

Also recognize that gathering this data and truly understanding the needs of the community takes time, sometimes lots of it. As the community shifts, families move in and out, and organizational leadership or mission take different directions, the needs will shift. It can take years to even begin to get a full picture of the needs of the community, but each conversation and identified need will contribute to that growing body of knowledge.

Step two: Identifying outcomes

After you have identified the need, you will need to narrow in on the specific outcomes you are hoping to achieve. These outcomes may be tied to the organic needs of the community, or may be the outcomes determined by a funder or policy.

In the most effective programs, goals and outcomes are directly tied to what families would like to see happen, as well as what the organization wants to offer. Often those two sets of goals are not all that different—but it can take intentional conversations to recognize that families and organizations are trying to get to the same place. Identifying outcomes and how they are tied to needs can be a great place for staff and families to join together on joint committees or strategic planning teams.

It's important to define what success will look like for you and your partners, in whatever programs or strategies you implement. Identifying outcomes and goals is not only good for funders—using data around outcomes to drive programming can help organizations be more efficient with their budgets, track efforts, and see how each of the steps they take moves towards addressing needs. Additionally, outcomes can help partners see progress, and take pride in small achievements accomplished along the way.

Posting outcomes and keeping them in mind, determining actions, and moving into implementation of ideas will serve as a reminder of why you do the work. Keeping outcomes manageable and specific to each effort will give staff and families motivation to do the work that moves towards reaching them.

Break up outcomes into manageable and realistic goals over time. While thriving partnerships and successful children might be the end goal, what outcomes can be reached this quarter, this semester, or this year?

How it all fits

Think about outcomes as the desired result of the work that you are doing. If families express a need for support that can help increase attendance at school, your outcome might be that all students will reach attendance rates of 85% for the year. The actions you take, and the events you plan should be focused on building the capacity of families and staff to work together to reach this outcome.

reflection

What strategies do you use to identify families' needs?

What challenges do you face when identifying outcomes?

Gathering family input: design thinking and human-centered design

Drawing on the fields of design and innovation, design thinking and human-centered design offer organizations a structured way to partner with families to gain a clearer understanding of all of the intricacies that shape a community. These are processes you can use to determine the needs of the families in your community and the outcomes you hope to achieve.

Human-centered design encourages us to put people at the forefront of any experience we might consider for them. Before we think about test scores and attendance at events, we should think about the human represented by each of those numbers in boxes, or names on the sign-in sheet. There are many reasons test scores may be high or low, many reasons families may or may not show up to the events we plan. Each of those reasons vary from child to child and family to family.

According to *The Field Guide to Human-Centered Design*, "Human-centered design isn't a perfectly linear process...you'll move through three main phases: Inspiration, Ideation, and Implementation. By taking these three phases in turn, you'll build deep empathy with the communities and individuals you're designing for." Using human-centered design strategies, an organization might organize a space and time for stakeholders from all parts of the community to come together. This gathering can include staff from the organization, local community leaders, and most importantly, families. You might have someone who is trained in design thinking to lead the group, or you may be pulling strategies to implement yourself. Whatever option you choose, the strategies that are employed to shape conversations help everyone in the room begin to understand the needs of the whole, and what the threads are that connect them all. Each individual can identify their place in the web of connection, and the group will begin to understand cause and effect as well. It puts all of the perspectives on the table and opens new lenses.

"Human-centered design offers problem solvers of any stripe a chance to design with communities, to deeply understand the people they're looking to serve, to dream up scores of ideas, and to create innovative new solutions rooted in people's actual needs."

– The Field Guide to Human-Centered Design

When a program or strategy might not have worked as hoped or planned, it can sometimes be explained by a mismatch between the perceived need and the actual need. Organizing the information-gathering process using human-centered design can support you in connecting with stakeholders to deeply understand the need, and apply whatever solution your group decides is most likely to achieve successful results. For example, a preschool might frequently have children who are complaining of hunger throughout the day. Perhaps the school thought that they could solve the problem by providing more snacks at school. When they talked with families, however, they realized that the deeper need was access to healthy, affordable food in the community. After the preschool understands the root of the issue, they can pivot their strategy to address hunger in a way that is more responsive, effective, and sustainable.

The focus of human-centered design is on empathy, ambiguity, and openness to trying new solutions to address challenges, soliciting ideas, feedback, alternatives, insights and discoveries from start to finish. After reflecting on the initial information, participants generate a single solution and test it out. This allows for customization and creates a wide path for growth. If the chosen solution doesn't work, it is easier to go back to the drawing board because other ideas are already there, waiting to be deployed.

This approach reminds us that, in order to understand human behavior, we have to put people first. Putting people first means investing in a relationship and giving it time to flourish. It means being genuine. And it requires us to stop focusing

from the field

Ascend at the Aspen Institute worked with a school district to use a "co-design" approach to create a family-led initiative that addressed needs that families had identified in the community. Instead of informing parents of an improvement plan, the school turned the decision over to parents. They asked: "With $15,000, how would you improve the schools?" Parents made suggestions and then helped choose the project to be funded. The result was a community-run mentoring program. The real outcome was deeper family engagement because parents felt heard and valued.

Anticipating problems

Part of laying the groundwork for any new idea or plan is thinking about what potential problems might need to be addressed. While you can't predict all of them, just as you can't predict all barriers families may face with engaging, it is not helpful to go into a new initiative without thinking about the issues that may come up. By identifying potential roadblocks—whether those are administrative, capacity related, or budgetary—your organization can be prepared to move into corrective action quickly, reducing the time spent wondering what to do next. There will still be moments of high stress or confusion when things go awry, but knowing that you have planned ahead can provide emotional strength to move forward with new ideas into unknown territory.

exclusively on the numbers when we launch innovative solutions that involve other humans. When we do, we may be surprised to see how much those numbers are impacted in positive ways.

Staff: relationships and rapport

As we have discussed more deeply in other chapters, engagement efforts work best when everyone in the organization believes in the efforts.

Part of the initiative you might need to take in your organization is to build staff buy-in. We've discussed professional development opportunities and providing staff with information about the positive outcomes of family engagement. Winning the hearts and minds of staff and families, however, and getting everyone excited about engagement, will take more. Your relationships with staff members will be the key to getting engagement efforts off the ground. You may need to be the one to initiate the development of those trusting partnerships with staff. At least in the beginning, it may fall on you to take the lead in building the bridge to staff buy-in.

While there are strategies that build staff buy-in as a group, you might also find yourself having one-on-one conversations with individuals to learn more about their thoughts, values, and barriers to engagement efforts. These conversations can help you to connect with peers around common topics, without making assumptions, being right, or winning. We can come away with mutual understanding—even if we still disagree. Maybe you are able to provide a new thought or experience around the benefits of engagement they had not considered before. Maybe they can do the same for you. When we start to have these conversations, attitudes can change. And then behaviors. And then interactions.

Getting engagement processes off the ground will come much easier when staff members join engagement efforts. Think about taking the initiative in the ways that you engage staff. The interpersonal connections you build will help foster enthusiasm and support within your organization.

from the field

In Braving the Wilderness: The Quest for True Belonging and the Courage to Stand Alone, author and social scientist Brené Brown emphasizes the importance of conversations that seek common ground as a starting point, that neutralize fear, and that allow strong emotions to be expressed, without escalating the situation. She encourages learning about others' perspectives, listening to understand (rather than to agree or disagree) and finding creative, forward-facing ways to transform conflict.

reflection

How has your organization adapted solutions to the needs and feedback of families?

Reflect on a conversation you've had with a colleague about family engagement work. How did that shift your perspective?

Imagination, responsivity, and creative solutions

It might be overwhelming to think about the immense needs that exist in every community, and maybe even more so when you think about the specific needs in your organization. However, each of these needs also provides an opportunity for change and growth, which is exciting! As you think about how to address the needs in your community, you might consider tried-and-true strategies, or you might use the information you've gathered from the community to create innovate solutions to specific challenges. This will require planning, thought, and intentional action, as well as initiative.

Innovation: try something new!

We can never know which solutions may be effective until we try. What challenges are unique to your organization? What's something new you haven't tried yet? What is a new twist on an old strategy?

Creative Problem Solving

One Parents as Teachers innovation adopted a unique approach to address common challenges in home visiting: they moved visits to a virtual platform using live, interactive videoconferencing. This unique design of service delivery allows parent educators to "visit" with families in the comfort of their own home. Although the innovation was originally designed to reach those who live far away from a program, virtual home visitors have discovered, through the development of the innovation, that it has the potential to accommodate the needs of many other parents for whom receiving home visits presents a challenge. For one family in particular, the virtual platform was the only way that they could receive the services they desperately wanted. The family's young daughter had a complex medical history that restricted who could come into the home. Because of the innovative thinking of Parents as Teachers and the ability of this affiliate to implement services through virtual visits, families with all types of needs or preferences are able to receive home visiting.

Schools and organizations are constantly developing new approaches to the same challenge, or new approaches to the new challenges that pop up every day. Professionals all over the country are using their creativity to address challenges to accessibility and service delivery, both to individual families and community wide.

One example of this is a Parents as Teachers program that was having difficulty scheduling a visit with a family during a time when both mom and dad were able to be there. The parent educator understood the value of dad also being engaged in the visit. Instead of opting to just visit with mom because it was easier, the parent educator decided to have the visits during the dad's lunch hour so that he could video chat and be a part of the conversation. The parent educator was not afraid of diving into a new strategy to address the need of working around dad's schedule, and the family was thankful that both parents could be engaged.

There are many reasons why a parent might not be able to be present at an event, conference, or meeting—they are deployed with the military, live in a different state or country, or travel a lot for work. You might think about how using technology can help you to integrate all sorts of family members into experiences around the child's education.

According to educational expert Joanna Gellar, another innovative response that has been adopted in some school districts to address a widespread need is the idea of cultural brokers. In some communities with a large immigrant populations, cultural brokers are responsible for outreach to parents. These mediators or collaborators earn trust by helping families navigate the system and offering opportunities for interaction.

Cultural brokers were an integral part of the family engagement plan in one school district in Rhode Island that received an Investing in Innovation or i3 grant from the U.S. Department of Education—to develop an early childhood education culture where parents felt welcomed, valued, respected, connected, and competent. The families that were most marginalized—including families of students with individualized education plans and those with limited English proficiency—participated in activities in greater numbers thanks to the project. Moreover, the level of trust between the cultural brokers and teachers was high, opening a new pathway for teachers to learn about their students.

These are just a few of the countless examples of innovative ways to address needs in communities across the country. One of these might jump out at you as a fit for your community, others may spark a whole new idea. Maybe none of these

Strong Fathers-Strong Families founder Mike Hall was a teacher and principal when he heard, over and over, that dads just weren't going to be engaged in their children's education, no matter what anyone did. Hall recognized the importance of fathers being engaged in their child's education, and the importance of schools letting fathers know they wanted them there. He left the schools to develop something innovative—a program designed with dads, for dads—that today is successfully engaging fathers in hundreds of schools across the country. Using his personal knowledge of fatherhood, along with research and input from other professionals, he created events that are focused on academics, but are built around the ways that dads typically engage with their children. What he has found is, even after the events, fathers continue to be engaged, as they are more comfortable with the school or organization. These schools are also learning what types of strategies work best to engage fathers, and are able to apply them to other events and activities as well.

fits a need that your community is experiencing. Wherever you are in developing ideas to address needs and reach outcomes, initiative is about gathering the data, taking the leap, and trying something new.

Small gestures

Not all needs are large and looming, or require grandiose plans to address them. When beginning to lay a foundation for sustainable engagement and partnerships, one place that often experiences the highest needs are the relationships between staff and families. To build these relationships you can start small, with simple gestures that don't take a lot of time or effort. Little things, like smiling at someone every day, or making a phone call you normally wouldn't, are a great place to jump in when other initiatives feel daunting.

When Karla Kush became principal of a middle school in Madison, Nebraska, her approach to the job was informed by many years of previous experience as a school counselor. Kush encouraged her teachers and staff to "communicate with families like you would with anybody else." This included texting personal messages about meaningful moments with students—good and bad.

Kush also empowered her athletic director to send coaches on home visits to talk about expectations for participating in sports. As a result, the coaches could leverage their new relationships with parents if student athletes missed practice without an excuse, or if low grades threatened their eligibility.

Part of getting started might simply be building a relationship with a parent who has had a difficult time connecting with anyone in the organization or school. Get to know them, find out why it's been a challenge. Encourage other staff to do the same. This might require you to challenge some grievances from the past, to reach out to those who you might be avoiding reaching out to. You need these families to be engaged just as much as you need the ones you see every day, and enjoy talking with. In fact, they might hold the answers you have been looking for.

Small gestures like these can be one of the most impactful ways to demonstrate initiative—and they do not require a large commitment of resources. Other low-cost strategies include smiling when parents walk in the door, changing signage to be more friendly, and providing a forum where parents can express themselves. When parents sense your earnestness, they will continue to engage, even if you are still working through the "big" strategies.

These relationships might provide your best ideas, as families are willing to partner with you and share their knowledge and perspectives. They also might be the boost that you need to push out a new idea or attempt to try something new.

Organizational support

While small gestures do not necessarily use a lot of resources or require permissions to do, some of your more innovative ideas may need a bit of organizational backing. They might require time and some amount of a budget allocation. Getting started also might require a lot of trust and flexibility as new ideas come to the table, and then go out into the community. Leadership will need to be comfortable with some initiatives starting and failing, knowing that the lessons learned along the way will inform the next attempt.

Most likely, if you are in a position of leadership and are reading this book, you are already thinking about family engagement in innovative ways, and are recognizing that staff and families need to be able to think together to push boundaries and move children towards success. If you are not in a position of leadership, you might be building the argument for why innovative solutions and flexible thinking are the way to address the needs of family engagement. Whatever your role, don't be afraid to be creative, and lean into new ways of thinking about long-existing needs.

reflection

What small gestures or low-cost strategies do you already use to demonstrate initiative?

What's a new technique or creative solution you would like to try in your organization?

Turning failure into opportunity

Family engagement is hard work. You are taking on a transformation that is unscripted and risky, and takes a lot of time. As you may have already experienced, failure happens—and it might happen often. When you have a growth mind-set, those failures will begin to change shape. You learn a lot from them. You may host what feels like a "failed" workshop that only has a few participants, but it could also be a success in terms of getting to know those parents a lot better, increasing their chances of continuing to engage.

Turning each failure into a learning opportunity will be a challenge, but will ultimately lead to better outcomes for families and children. Someone has to start. Maybe it is you. Maybe it is a community member. Maybe it is a team of dedicated people from all sectors related to the child. Each of these opportunities provides a new chance for creativity to flourish and change to happen.

You might find that, if you keep a mind-set focused on finding new solutions, you'll discover a whole new way of looking at challenges and opportunities. You might find information and inspiration in places you never thought to look before.

The research, connections, and examples we've discussed in this chapter set the stage for diving in—and getting started is half the battle! In the next chapter, we'll take a look at the other half: persistence.

Initiative

Transformation needs a starting point. Taking the initiative means listening and learning from the community about where to start. We bring our best creative thinking to the table.

moving forward

There are many aspects to initiative. Take a moment to reflect on the previous chapter and think about which ideas, strategies, or pieces of initiative are strongest, and which require growth.

> **Identifying needs**

> **Identifying outcomes**

> **Gathering family input: design thinking and human-centered design**

> **Innovation: try something new**

> **Small gestures**

> **Organizational support**

We're strong on this:

We're so-so at this:

We're working on it:

Persistence

When it comes to increasing family engagement, getting started is often the hardest part. Still, you may be asking: What happens after things get started? What if I face hurdle after hurdle in my efforts to cultivate intentional partnerships? Of course keeping the end goal in mind will help along the way, but family engagement is not always as easy as it sounds.

Each of us keeps working towards engagement and partnership because we believe what the research tells us: that it leads to better outcomes for children. We believe that if we do the work to build partnerships, families and children in our communities will benefit as well. Persistence must be supported by a little bit of optimism; all partners in the process need to believe that what they are trying to do will not only work, but will improve the world around them.

Moving through setbacks and frustrations is hard, especially when it can take years for large-scale successes to take hold. Sometimes it's easy to become discouraged when the small successes—even when we know how much they matter—still don't feel like enough to overcome the failures.

The work we do with families is not all that different from the work we do with children. Take a moment to reflect on a scenario that may be familiar to many of you. Suppose that a student is pushing your buttons. how do you respond? Middle-school principal Karla Kush calls these "2-by-10 kids." Kush, a former counselor, instructs her teachers and staff in Madison, Nebraska, to build relationships with these children very systematically. "We are going to meet with that one student two minutes a day for 10 days," she says. "We're going to intentionally go to that student and say, 'Hey, how was your day so far?' or 'What did you do over the weekend?'" In short, they respond by spending time with the student.

What is the result of this response? "The behaviors we weren't liking have disappeared," Kush says. "There are a couple who are still challenging, but they have more better days than last year."

Kush's strategy is deceptively simple. It consists of brief but frequent and intentional connections repeated over time—measured initially in minutes, then days, then years. It incorporates some of the values covered in other chapters, like compassion, initiative, and generosity.

We can see parallels between Kush's approach and the process of engaging families. Persistence is a critical factor in both. At times, engagement is centered around getting initiatives within the organization up and running, repeatedly, over time. At other times, it looks like staff continuing to push forward with strategies even when they know that immediate outcomes aren't likely. From another perspective, persistence looks like a parent pushing, frequently and intentionally, to become part of the system. We may see staff members who keep trying new and different ways to engage that one family they can't quite connect with. The "2-by-10" method is just one of the many examples of how we can break big tasks down into smaller, more manageable daily interactions.

Keeping the big picture in mind is a key motivator for both individuals and organizations. We are more likely to persist when we have an end goal that drives our actions, that supports us as we keep moving forward (and probably backwards a little as well). For many early childhood professionals and educators, the big picture goal is that each family will be a partner in their child's education, from birth through college. For organizations, schools, and early childhood centers, the big picture goal may be to effectively team with parents to create a path to success for all children. Parents and caregivers most likely have these same big-picture goals as well.

What is success?

The five-year, $15 million "Investing in Family Engagement Project" in Philadelphia public schools served more than 5,500 children via after-school programming. In the final evaluation of this enormous undertaking, researchers at the Wisconsin Center for Education Research and the University of Wisconsin-Madison said they were "unable to show whether such a program could indeed effect [sic] overall positive change and school turnaround. The overall research results were null—no effects found."

Rather than throwing in the towel, admitting defeat, and quietly moving away from the work, they detailed the contextual factors that came into play. These included: high family mobility, lack of stakeholder input from the start, misaligned expectations, insufficient pilot testing, competing institutional influences, inadequate identification of resources before implementation, funding constraints that limited flexibility, and a lack of time for building relationships and tailoring programs. They reported that, "the lessons we learned over five years are powerful and worth considering by anyone trying to initiate and scale up family engagement programs in challenged schools and districts."

Like the researchers, we believe that successful engagement efforts are not necessarily those that work perfectly from the start and don't ever "fail". We encourage each of you to look to the small successes along the way. In the example above, successes included strong collaborative work by the implementation team, continued participation by all schools, creation of more than 40 outreach products, and strong awareness of the project and its goals (more than 89 percent of families surveyed at the schools knew about the program).

Setting smaller goals for success along the way can support motivation for moving towards that end goal, and makes setbacks more manageable. You might also find that your definition of success changes along the way. Like the researchers above, you may realize that what you started to believe was "success" was not actually the whole story. Eventually, as partnerships continue, you will move closer to the end goal of better outcomes for children and their families.

Taking the long view

Maintaining the optimism that drives effort at the start can be one of the biggest challenges for everyone—staff and families alike. Outcomes do not happen in a single day, and they may not be obvious even when you reach them. When asked to pinpoint a time she saw the results of her work, one parent educator gave this example in a PATNC survey: "Today as I was working with a single parent, she referenced information I had shared with her about a year ago, and how she had used that to help her make a decision about her child. [She] stated, 'I know what you said was in the abstract and general, but when I planned our holiday, it came to my mind.' I felt like she had understood me and my role—and used that understanding to make her child's life better." What this parent educator realized was that she wasn't aware of her impact on the family's well-being, because she was only seeing a snapshot of the family's life.

It can be frustrating to not see progress when we rely on knowing successes to provide motivation. Remind yourself that these small moments of impact are happening, even when they aren't highly visible.

Margaret Caspe, Director of Research and Professional Learning at the Global Family Research Project, is intentional about describing family engagement as a process rather than a one-time event. If we can think of it this way, from the beginning, we are less likely to be defeated by the forward and backward movement of the work. One benefit of taking a long-term approach is that there are many opportunities for information to flow back and forth between partners. When things don't work, there are also many points to start over. During times of transition, there may be new chances to replace old patterns of communication and negative experiences with newer, more positive ones.

reflection

What big goal motivates you to do the work to engage families?

What have you noticed about the factors that cause discouragement as you do this work?

Addressing challenges

Reducing barriers and welcoming all stakeholders to join as partners in the efforts to reach higher outcomes for kids is a constant task. In the surveys we've conducted for this book, hundreds of family support professionals and parent educators shared the best and the worst of their family engagement experiences. They reported being overwhelmed by families' needs, and discouraged by low turnout at events, or no-shows at meetings. They were unprepared for many "asks" from their employers and stymied by a shortage of transportation options. They lacked time and resources to carry out their ideas, and faced struggles around sharing power. They were unsure of how to draw out more apprehensive families, or how to defuse tense situations.

We have addressed many barriers and challenges in this book, and each of you is aware of the challenges specific to your community. Underlying many of the challenges is the fact that we each have our own beliefs about family engagement and partnership. None of us, families or staff, come into our relationships with each other with clean slates. All of our past experiences contribute to how we view and experience both challenges and successes.

Disengagement

Each of you reading this book works in your own unique community, with its own characteristics and ways of being. Many of you, we would guess, are also working in communities that have something in common: a history of disengagement. Disengagement is a complex process—one that can take a long time to reverse. In many ways, it is a process that parallels a high-school student deciding to end the trek toward graduation. As noted by America's Promise Alliance, "dropping out of school does not occur overnight but is a gradual process of disengagement that can be interrupted when communities, schools, and families work together to identify when and why their young people do not succeed in school, and to ensure young people, especially those most at risk, receive the supports they need." Notably, family engagement is listed near the top among the factors that can mitigate dropout rates—which of course compounds the challenge if that's also an area in which a school or community is struggling.

> Remember that families present views and experiences are influenced by past experiences with school, with people "like you", or with whatever else reminds them of what you are trying to do.

Families' previous experiences

As we discussed in "Trust", the negative impact of past interactions and experiences with schools can be incredibly fresh, making them challenging to work through. Individuals come to you carrying their previous experiences with your agency or organization, in addition to their experiences with similar institutions in the past. They may have had challenging interactions as a student themselves that now impact how they engage with their child's school. They may have had a teacher they didn't get along with, and that relationship may have set the pattern for all future interactions with school staff.

As a result of these interactions over time, families may begin to disengage. Patterns of disengagement can run deep through communities where negative patterns of interaction have been established.

Don't give up on these families, even if it might seem like they are fighting you every step of the way or ignoring your every attempt to connect. While it would be unproductive to hound families in an attempt to get them to listen or show up, we encourage persisting with genuine, compassionate attempts to connect. These difficult attempts can feel draining, but when a genuine connection is finally made, it might give you motivation to keep going.

Previous experiences of staff

Families aren't the only ones who are bringing their previous experiences with them. Staff members—yourself included—bring along memories and emotions from working with families. These might manifest in general expectations that families will behave in stereotypical ways, or they might involve a specific family that has presented an ongoing challenge in the past that has become personal.

In addition, the experiences staff members have *not* had can be a barrier to connecting. This is often viewed in terms of racial or socioeconomic differences, but there are many other life experiences that impact our ability to connect over shared experiences. Perhaps a teacher lives in a rural setting but works in an urban one. Maybe you're helping to integrate a new family from another country, and you have never had a similar experience. Harvard Graduate School of Education author Leah Schafer points out that recognizing and learning about the "funds of knowledge" all families bring is tremendously helpful for staff as they strive to take a strengths-based approach to building partnerships regardless of previous experiences.

Sometimes it can feel easier to blame families for a lack of connection than to acknowledge that our own views and assumptions may be negatively impacting our interactions. Our biases may create a situation that makes it very challenging to engage authentically. It doesn't always feel good, but exploring our individual roles in creating and maintaining barriers for families is an important part of growing in the work.

If you've struggled to form a positive relationship with a parent or family member in the past, identifying small goals can make overcoming these situations feel less daunting. Maybe just start with a smile and a friendly acknowledgment rather than avoiding a parent you've had a negative interaction with when you see them coming.

Caspe reminds us, each interaction is a new opportunity to redirect relationships through frequent, repeated contact. Don't be discouraged when there are no immediate changes. Redirecting relationships that are rooted in past experiences is a slow process. It may require considerable time and energy from everyone, but your work will be more impactful when the time is taken to lay a strong groundwork.

from the field

Teen parents present a unique set of considerations that we have not touched on deeply in this book. A Parents as Teachers program that served teen parents was having difficulty connecting with its participants. The parent educators who visited the teens in their homes came together and had a conversation about the power of being present in not only the teens' communities, but specifically in the parts of the community that were a part of daily life for the young parents.

After that, the parent educators spent time connecting with the teens in different ways. They stopped by the local clinic to talk to staff, and then chatted with the parents who happened to be there. They went to get fast food from the restaurants where the parents worked. They began putting themselves in situations that allowed for chance meetings, and these chance meetings demonstrated to the teens that the parent educators really were trying to understand them—and also that their parent educators were a part of their community.

These strategies took a lot more effort than just showing up for visits as scheduled with the families, but they also paid off. These teens began showing up more regularly for their visits, and they were ultimately willing to engage more deeply with the parent educators as they came to trust them.

Adaptation and flexibility

A large part of persistence includes a willingness to be adaptable and flexible, to stay true to the end goal while being willing to try various strategies to get there. This is clear when you look at organizations doing family engagement work in varied ways. Even though we might all have the same end goal in mind, the path we choose to get there can look drastically different. Not only does this vary by organization, it varies based on the population and life experience of your target community. Caspe points out that engaging adolescent parents may require strategies that look a little different than methods for engaging older parents. Pathways may change as children get older—entering kindergarten looks very different from entering middle school, and so does engaging families in each of those life stages.

Engagement also varies between and within families in each of those stages. Families often have a preferred means of engaging, and successful partnerships depend on being able to identify how to serve them. In an interview with *Seattle Times*, family engagement expert Karen Mapp notes that even when you are working through what a partnership with a specific family looks like, the important thing is to let parents know how essential they are to the work. "A lot of times, parents don't hear that. They don't hear that 'we can't do this without you'. They hear, 'We got this. Just drop your child off.'..we don't let them know that we do need them and at least need their advice or knowledge of their child, and we have to tell them that face to face." Remind parents that we need them, value them, and want to work together to find what works for everyone.

Adaptability does not just mean moving from one thing to the next, in quick succession, to find a strategy that "works." It can take years to produce the desired outcomes from a single strategy, especially when attempting to partner with families or staff that are hesitant to engage. Balance persistence in working towards your long-term strategy with giving yourself freedom to adapt. Change course when you have to, but with intentionality and communication with your partners about what is working and what is not.

Transitions

One particular moment in time when engagement can either dip or surge is during transitions. As families move from an early care setting into school, or from home visiting into early care, or even from one grade to another at the same school, they go through a transition from one set of engagement strategies to another. These transitions force everyone to learn something new. Families need to learn how the new school or center engages, and schools and centers need to figure out how to best partner with new families.

Caspe points out that the systematic identification of transition points ahead of time is key for handling change successfully. The summer before kindergarten is one widely recognized transition point. However, it can be a huge challenge to reach families early enough to partner with them during their child's transition into school. This is why effective outreach during the kindergarten enrollment period is so important in establishing meaningful connections. Families who participate in transition processes are also more encouraged to take leadership roles later on, demonstrating the impact of engaging early.

Engagement in the home

Early childhood providers are known for engaging families in a comprehensive way, often because children are in their care for shorter periods of time, and they rely on families to continue the learning that is started at the center. They also might be providing services within the family's home, which provides a natural point of engagement.

The transition into engagement at school can be stressful for families who are used to more comprehensive communication. The level of expectation families bring can also be stressful for staff as they are attempting to implement their own ideas of engagement. Communication with families at this point about expectations that both staff and families have can help reduce frustration by avoiding more intense conversations in moments of stress.

Transitions between organizations can be less stressful if families can expect similar engagement patterns across organizations. You may consider reaching out to other agencies or schools your students may be transferring from to discuss strategies they've used, what worked, and what didn't. Partnerships between various agencies can support a more comprehensive experience for families as they transition.

Each of the values outlined in this book requires continual effort to build upon and strengthen. We know that family engagement is a never-ending process, and that there is no finish line.

It can also be beneficial to talk with families to find out what is happening at different organizations and schools in your community from their perspective. These insights can support you in creating a more streamlined experience of engagement from early childhood through the high school years.

Remember, too, that transitions don't just occur between schools, or early childhood to school. Once children are in a formalized setting they are typically grouped by age, and may be transitioning from teacher to teacher in different classrooms. Use the same strategies discussed above to support students as they transition from room to room. Conversations with your colleagues can lead to insights about the strategies they use, and can take the guesswork out of relationships with families that are new to you, but whom they

Expectations

Each shift in patterns of engagement can create misunderstandings and frustrations if expectations are unclear. Open communication about expectations from all partners in the transition process can play a large role in supporting all those involved.

know well and have established clear patterns of partnership with. This will reduce stress for staff and families as they see that engagement looks similar across staff.

Even though transitions offer plenty of opportunities for engagement to drop, they also offer many opportune moments for engagement to thrive. Transitions are an opportunity to engage families as they seek support, and begin to see what their child's new environment means for them.

reflection

As you think about the challenges that you have had (or expect to have) when persisting in your work to engage families, what do you notice about the work that families are doing at the same time?

What challenges might families say require the most persistence from them as they seek to engage with you?

Continuing on

The unending nature of family engagement work means that there will inevitably be challenges along the way. These challenges might be large and obvious. They might be small but accumulate until they form something that feels overwhelming. While it is important to be realistic about what lies ahead, it is equally important to maintain a positive outlook. Try not to waste energy worrying about roadblocks that might not even exist, or ones you cannot control.

There will often be setbacks in the work of engaging and creating partnerships with families; it would be unrealistic to say it will be a smooth journey. Those setbacks can originate in the organization, in the families, or in the community, but they are not the end of the road.

Rely on those partnerships that you have worked hard to create to push through the setbacks and celebrate the successes. Relish the small successes, the smile that you never have gotten before, the one person who showed up to a group, the parent night that had five parents at it this time instead of just one.

This work needs people like you. People who recognize that challenges lie ahead yet still look forward to the work. People who are willing to be flexible and steadfast in working towards the bigger goal, a goal that you recognize families and schools and communities all share.

Even if our successes are no bigger than a gold star up on the wall, there will always be rewards that can remind you of why it is you keep persisting.

Persistence

Transformation is hard work. It takes time for changes to become established, for setbacks to be overcome, and for those who are steadfast to be seen as assets.

moving forward

There are many aspects to persistence. Take a moment to reflect on the previous chapter and think about which ideas, strategies, or pieces of persistence are strongest, and which require growth.

> **Taking the long view**   > **Previous experiences of staff**

> **Disengagement**   > **Transitions**

> **Families' previous experiences** > **Continuing on**

We're strong on this:

We're so-so at this:

We're working on it:

Sustainability

As communities and families continue to evolve, it takes a great deal of time and effort to engage families in partnerships that improve outcomes for children. Take the time to lay a long-term foundation for engagement practices, built on a shared commitment and sustainable solutions, that will continue to effect lasting change for families in your community.

The one factor that is a constant when working with children and families is change. Children grow, families move in and out of communities, staff move to new positions—yet the work of engaging families remains. Building a comprehensive, flexible, and successful family engagement strategy takes a lot of work. Sometimes it can feel like starting over, year after year, as new families and new staff come on board, or as organizations shift approaches and programs. Focusing on sustainable  practices from the beginning will lay the groundwork for successful engagement over time, through whatever transitions might arise.

The conversations echoed throughout this book—focusing on values, goals, and partnering with families—create a foundation for sustainable family engagement. These conversations are where your organization, the families in your community, and the individuals with whom you partner will start to establish patterns that can achieve results—while still allowing flexibility for inevitably changing dynamics. In this chapter, the focus is on putting it all together and thinking about how each value might contribute to building a sustainable path for engagement efforts in your organization.

Building an effective long-term framework

Our goal at Parents as Teachers is that families will become partners with family support professionals and educators from the very beginning, and that these partnerships will build sustainable engagement that propel children into successful futures. Whether you share this precise goal or not, we would imagine that the reason you are reading this book is because you are working, as an organization, towards a similar outcome. We know that this goal is lofty, and that it may take months or years to get to a place where we feel that intentional partnerships are being built in our programs.

We also know, as do you, that the work of building engagement strategies that work in the long run is never complete. While short-term goals may vary immensely, and shift with changes in the organization, having a framework in place creates a path for navigating these shifts and changes. Taking the time to observe and communicate with families and staff around goals and

Family engagement—it's here to stay

Policies that require family engagement are solidifying the fact that it is here to stay. Organizations are required to meet certain engagement benchmarks to retain funding—whether at the federal, state, or local level, whether public or private—and it's becoming more and more common for them to be required to have a family engagement strategy. Some programs, such as Head Start or the Federal Maternal, Infant, and Early Childhood Home Visiting Program, offer detailed guidance for how to develop an engagement strategy within different facets of their work. Even within these guidelines there are many variations in implementation strategies. In others, there are no specific guidelines, and it is up to the organization or school to think broadly about how to create sustainable frameworks.

values will lead to the selection of strategies that are most likely to yield successful outcomes. Even if you don't get the outcomes you hoped for, a framework based on values—holding the end goal in mind—along with the determination to go through the process again, can support the willingness try a new approach.

This is why we haven't simply provided you with a list of strategies that you might try. Instead, we are hoping to support your underlying thinking as you develop a comprehensive, intentional framework for family engagement. Once you have the framework, the strategies can be placed and replaced as needed according to the variables, at any given point in time.

Creating sustainable engagement efforts requires a shift in how an organization functions—a shift in culture. To build a truly sustainable framework for family engagement, many parts and people need to be considered. A few factors that we have already focused on in previous chapters, include:

- Program design
- Staff and hiring
- Roles and responsibilities
- Feedback from families

There are some additional key considerations, listed below, that we have not covered in-depth in earlier chapters. While this is not a comprehensive list, you will want to think about these areas while working towards a long-term framework for intentional partnerships with families:

- **Leadership buy-in:** Funding efforts, policy, providing the time and motivation to staff—all of these resources are provided by leadership that not only "gets" engagement efforts, but prioritizes them. It's not just staff that feel supported when leadership commits to making family engagement part of a systemic shift. When it is clear they are supported, families feel empowered to shape programs and services or influence policies and systems.

- **Motivation for participants:** Have you had conversations with families about why they do or do not participate? Creating patterns of engagement that last requires constantly having conversations to identify what keeps families coming back, or what gets them in the door. While extrinsic motivation might get them there, finding out what needs your organization is satisfying for them will help foster intrinsic motivation as well. The latter is the most likely to stick in the long term.

A word about incentives

Providing items of financial value in exchange for attendance has its pros and cons. Expert Judy Ryan notes that while it can indeed boost the number of parents who come to an event, it also implies people will only contribute or participate productively when there is "something in it for them" in a material sense. Research has found that humans' commitment to the very behavior you want them to continue is reduced over time if they rely solely on material incentives.

However, incentives are not always harmful to engagement. One example of a well-designed incentive is to give away books at a literacy event. Incentives like this not only encourage families to attend, but also incentivize interaction with their child. Providing families with an opportunity for a positive interaction, useful and relevant information, and concrete support are all more useful in building the intrinsic motivation that contributes to sustainable engagement.

- **Planning and strategy:** How does family engagement fit into the strategic planning for the organization? Being able to provide connections—from activities related to engagement, like letting parents lead initiatives, to outcomes, like kindergarten readiness—provides a rationale for why engagement should be included. Think of the long-term impact when trying to create sustainable change; is the organization offering "boutique projects" or random activities that look good on paper, but don't contribute to the organization's mission or strategic plan? Or are they looking to make real systemic change?

- **Accountability:** When laying the framework for engagement, there may be times when promises are made to families, or to staff, that do not end up coming to fruition. While this is a reality for any work, how those mishaps are handled can greatly impact whether families will be willing to join your organization for the long haul, or if they will feel let down and draw back. Both organizations and schools must have strategies in place to continuously be monitoring feedback, and ensuring that they are doing what they said they would. The partnership works best when open lines of communication from both sides hold each other accountable in reasonable ways.

reflection

Is there a place for family engagement in the strategic planning of your organization?

What are some of the short-term and long-term goals for family engagement in your organization?

Sustainable partnerships

Family engagement is built on partnerships, and requires both staff and families to work together to be successful. Just as families will move through your school, community organization, or early childhood program, staff will go through changes over time as well. Each of the values and practices that you have been reflecting on in the last nine chapters are wonderful in and of themselves, but rely on staff and families to implement them on a daily basis. Laying a foundation for family engagement means providing staff and family supports that they need to be effective in partnering.

Communicating with parents

Parents will be willing to engage with schools if they are given clear rationale and can see the benefits of engaging. Just as with staff, communicating the message around the importance of engaging, and how it fits within the context of their current roles and duties, makes it far more likely parents will be willing to engage.

How organizations communicate the purpose of engagement also dictates whether or not families will stay engaged over time. Communicating messages that parents should participate in events because it will "help" them, or that feel like instructions for how to do things at home, will not lead to sustainable patterns of engagement. On the other hand, if efforts are made to communicate to parents that organizations want to partner with them, to get to know them and support them as needed (not as dictated), then families will be more willing to enter into partnership. One school director set the stage for an effort to increase literacy at home by letting parents know she would make random phone calls in the evening to find out if they'd had time to read to their child that day. This was not a reminder call, and it didn't focus on families who were not likely to have read. She simply let the families fill her in on how things had gone that day. She then followed-up after the call to let the families know she appreciated their time—perhaps in the form of a thank-you note, or with a new book. The phone calls and her willingness to listen to the families' perspective created the basis for sustainable relationships with these families.

Getting, and keeping, families engaged

Just as with events and other efforts, opportunities for families to get and stay engaged are more sustainable if they are consistent. Reflect on a time when you were given the opportunity to provide feedback. Did a one-time survey make you want to reach out and continue to engage with an organization or company? Probably not. These one-off events to provide feedback are great, and are ways to gather a lot of data at once, but alone they are not sufficient to keep families coming back for more.

Consistently providing opportunities for families to get engaged and give feedback at multiple levels allows the organization to continue to understand the current needs of the families, and make adjustments as needed. The variety of ways and depths to get engaged also reinforces the messaging to families that you are invested in hearing their voices, no matter how much or little time they have to give. Establishing patterns for regular input, leadership opportunities, and feedback establishes families' roles as integral parts of the organization, not just now, but in the future. Some examples of opportunities to engage that may be consistently implemented are:

- **Family committees.** Advising, building awareness, and providing suggestions are all ways for staff and families to work side by side towards long-term goals. As committee members get more familiar with one another, and trust is established, organizations may begin to ask these committees to weigh in on major decisions, like hiring new staff. Over time, families' input can change the way services are delivered, making them more responsive to the community needs.

- **Feedback loops.** To create sustainable practices where families and staff alike feel valued in their role of giving feedback, suggestions must be implemented. If their suggestions are not feasible, that also needs to be addressed with families. When individuals feel like they are being respected and heard, they are more likely to continue to engage. These respectful discussions strengthen the partnership between families and staff, and demonstrate that when they have suggestions to offer, they will be taken into account by the organization. Establishing a culture of listening and responding sets families up to be engaged year after year.

- **Parent-run programs and events.** Offering parents opportunities to lead demonstrates a level of trust and respect that builds confidence in the partnership, and in themselves. When these opportunities are offered consistently, and become a natural part of the way the organization functions, families have more time to ease their way into involvement. That parent who doesn't feel ready to jump in right away might see others leading, and build up the confidence to take on roles over time.

Advocacy for sustainability

In the broader community, parents may be trained as leaders who take their message to government officials and policymakers, creating a lasting path for family engagement work in the broader community. Families also benefit from these advocacy efforts, strengthening skills that set them up for their own sustainable engagement. As families are engaged in advocacy in authentic ways, they become recognized as trusted sources of information, and build networks of influence within public realms.

from the field

Offering families consistent leadership opportunities requires staff to take a step back and trust the process. Bev Schumacher of Kentucky recalled a time when parents came up with a plan to decorate shirts for all of the students using paint. Because the paint dried more slowly than expected, "shirts were hanging all over the center. [It was a] nightmare of a project and the staff could not wait to be done with it." Meanwhile, one of the parents called the local TV station about the shirts, and a crew came out to film, complete with interviews of children about reading, which were then aired on TV. The moral of the story? "Parents sometimes have ideas that are really great, even if they don't seem like it at the time." Letting families implement their plans all the way through, even if you can't see what the finish line might look like, demonstrates a level of trust that makes families want to be a part of your organization.

Carve out the time for staff

Professionals who are tasked with engaging families have many more duties included in their roles besides family engagement work. Teachers work long hours. Often their time is split between classroom duties and professional commitments such as learning communities, professional development, special education meetings, and department meetings. Parent educators affiliated with home visiting models like Parents as Teachers balance their time planning visits, delivering services, recording information, and fulfilling other tasks like facilitating groups and researching resources in the community.

Implementing family engagement efforts, in whatever context you might find yourself, is hard work. Burnout is a very real and pressing issue for many individuals who work with children and families. This can be exacerbated when an individual doesn't feel supported in their work.

Leadership buy-in ties in closely with providing the supports necessary for staff to feel successful in partnering with families. As discussed in "Generosity", engagement and building intentional partnerships with families takes time, sometimes a lot of it. Staff who work with children are already pressed for time to fit in all of the other tasks. If engaging families feels like another responsibility added to their job description, with no time to do it, the risk of burnout and frustration rises.

Training

As we know, partnering with families does not come naturally to all family support professionals, educators, or service providers. Nor does partnering with staff come naturally to all parents. Professional development can be offered around what it means to partner with families in general, but tailoring trainings and development opportunities to reflect your families and communities will make it more likely that partnering becomes an integrated part of what your team does in the future.

Building on principles of adult learning

As highlighted by Kendall Zoller and Claudette Landry, adult learning theory states that we are more likely to retain information when we are able to make direct connections to our own work or lives. This applies to supporting both professionals and families. The more connections you can make during professional development to staff and families' lives, the more they will retain. Building capacity for engagement over time requires the retention of both knowledge and skills, as well as continual development.

At times there will be conflicts between the time and effort needed to engage families, and the time and effort that staff are able to give. Creating an environment where reflective supervision or other emotional supports are consistently available for staff to share their challenges and solutions will reduce staff turnover. Having low rates of turnover and a stable team make it much easier to create sustainable patterns of engagement. Families and staff get to know each other better, and staff come to embody the expectation and culture of engaging families.

To avoid engagement work feeling like an add-on to staff's other duties, the messaging around what engagement is and isn't is important. Frame the messaging as a shift in *how* the work is done. Engagement strategies should be integrating staff's skills and interests into the ways in which they engage families. Building the work into existing duties reduces strain on staff capacity and creates more opportunities for long-term success.

Staff that want to be a part of the organization or school because they feel supported are more likely to stay, and more likely to embrace the challenges and successes of family engagement together, in long-term, sustainable ways.

What consistent opportunities are available for family input, leadership, and feedback in your organization?

How does your organization allocate time for staff to engage with families?

Sustainable financial support

As we know all too well, creating new initiatives or frameworks costs money. Building relationships with families during the routine workday has little to no financial cost, but there are many peripheral expenses that can support or hinder the building of those relationships. Some of these are one-time costs, but investments like staff members' salaries require more consistent funding to be sustainable.

Expenditures like transportation and food can boost attendance at on-site events—ranging from open houses to parent-teacher conferences—and can be supported by partnerships with community agencies. These partnerships can be extremely valuable in securing free or low-cost food, supplies, and event spaces that do not put a large strain on the organization or school. For example, Kodiak Bible Church in Kodiak, Alaska, lets organizations that serve families use its facilities for free. "While the rooms aren't posh or decked out in the latest technology, the church's staff is always warm and welcoming," said one parent educator. "They check on us and make sure that we have what we need. And they don't get upset if something small breaks or gets used up. They want healthy families in the community too." Building partnerships like these not only makes families feel more comfortable, but they are also a great way to save funding that can keep the initiative going longer.

Even the most well-connected and resourceful organizations need reliable, consistent funding sources. These sources can include ongoing federal and state funding, as well as board-level support for local organizations like school districts, and service-oriented nonprofits. *Inside Philanthropy* author Caitlin Reilly points out that there are also many new sources of philanthropic funding that have "discovered" family engagement in recent years, on the heels of research illustrating its benefits for student outcomes. While these funding opportunities exist, organizations may need to dig deep to find them, and get creative in thinking about how the funding might be applied to various aspects of family engagement work. Funding opportunities won't always directly spell out that they are intended to be used in family engagement efforts.

In addition to external sources of funding, the sustainability of efforts relies on internal financial commitments as well. Delegating work to staff, or letting families plan an event but then providing no money to implement makes it clear that family engagement is not really a priority for the organization.

"If you truly value families' voices at the table, then you need to be willing to do what you can to get them there, and this may cost money. You might need to support with transportation, or provide meals, but showing that you are willing to help get them there also demonstrates that you value them enough to put your money there."

– Kate McGilly, *Director of Projects and Grant Management*, Parents as Teachers National Center

reflection

In what ways is your organization currently financially investing in family engagement efforts?

What potential or untapped sources of funding might be available for your organization's efforts?

The work that each individual organization is doing to create sustainable family engagement efforts in their own communities has a ripple effect on the larger education system. The work is never done, but creating sustainable frameworks lays a path for families and organizations to have a clear sense of where they are going, and to learn from where they have been.

The relationships you build with families will also begin to have a ripple effect within your own organization, as other families are able to observe what it looks like to partner with you. As more families become integrated partners, those partnerships come more naturally to the entire community; they become a part of what defines the organization. This reputation is what attracts the families and staff that continue to develop intentional parternships with families, creating a sustainable future for engagement.

Sustainability

Once we put in the work to get something going, we want it to be around for a while. Sustainability means always keeping the goal in mind: to build lasting partnerships.

moving forward

There are many aspects to sustainability. Take a moment to reflect on the previous chapter and think about which ideas, strategies, or pieces of sustainability are strongest, and which require growth.

> **Communicating with parents**
> **Getting, and keeping, families engaged**

> **Carve out the time for staff**
> **Sustainable financial support**

We're strong on this:

We're so-so at this:

We're working on it:

Conclusion

"We need to intentionally seek out those who are perpetually not at the table."

– Christy Roberts, Parent and *Implementation Support Manager,*
Parents as Teachers National Center

Putting the values into action

Family engagement is complex. It is influenced by each interaction that a family has with an organization, and with the individual staff members within an organization. It is also inherently personal. The relationships that are developed between families, organizations, and communities are the very basis on which engagement is built or erodes over time. Family engagement is a process with a continual trajectory for growth and development that looks different for each family, organization, and individual. You may be at any stage in the journey towards a comprehensive engagement initiative. You may be just beginning the conversation about why engagement even matters, or you may be looking to refine and strengthen the work that has already been happening for years.

Wherever your organization is in its journey, there is never an endpoint, never a time when you can say, "It's complete." The changing nature of the relationships at the heart of engagement ensures that the work is never done. There will always be a new group of young children coming in, and another group exiting, bringing or taking their families with them. Even in the face of this complex reality, you can set up the environment in which positive relationships form more naturally than before, where your values around family engagement start to travel by word of mouth from one generation of families to the next, and where your organization's reputation as a steadfast partner becomes unshakable.

It is difficult to shift the norms of engagement. Many organizations resist change because they are not sure how to define and manage true partnerships with families. Many families are hesitant because they have already experienced being pushed away or disengaged. But for every person who is disengaged, and every organization stuck in a rut, there is also a parent ready to reach out, and an individual within that organization ready to reciprocate.

Look to bolster family strengths, and tap into the reasons why families might engage with you. Get to know families in an authentic way. Do the same for staff. Help them to find the reason why they personally might want to dive into the work of engaging families, and guide individuals towards work that highlights their strengths. Do the same for yourself! Find the places where you feel you are able to make the biggest impact and where you can grow. When we can work to identify common ground, and recognize that the goals we are working towards are the same, the efforts feel less daunting.

Considerations for moving forward

We hope that these chapters have prepared you for productive initial conversations with your partners. As you begin to lay the foundation together, you can arrive at a shared understanding of the goals you hope to achieve, and how you will get there together.

As you take a step back and reflect on how you will move forward in building intentional partnerships, you might consider the following questions:

- How you will raise self-awareness within your colleagues about where they fall on the continuum of engagement, and where they are in the journey?

- Which people within the organization can give you a better sense of the overall environment via honest, open conversations?

- What new strategies might you wish to implement? Do they align with your partners' wishes? Keep in mind that the odds of success are much higher when everyone involved has input and can see the bigger picture.

- Are some of your "norms" of practice counterproductive to your overall efforts? Give yourself permission to end practices that might be making engagement more challenging for families or for yourself.

Understanding where you're going

Moving forward starts with conversations—talking with families and colleagues about where they find themselves on the continuum of engagement, understanding which values ring true for them, and which values they find the most challenging to embrace. Understand where your partners hope to be, and spend a bit of time gathering ideas about what success in family engagement means to them. You may be surprised at the answers you get. When we asked this question, the list of answers we received included: connection, curiosity, focus, cooperation, hope, happiness, caring, affection, cheerfulness, hugs, empowerment, high fives, smiles, balance, confidence, sharing, responsiveness, laughter, and "awesome big humans."

Each of these answers highlight the successes you can find along the way; embrace the small steps and the giant leaps forward. Find the small wins in the stories that are shared with you, and celebrate them! Learn from the failures and be willing to shift how and where you are going when things aren't turning out how you expected. Each of these successes and failures are a part of the process. Families might still be hesitant to lead despite supports and opportunities put in place; staff may still be hesitant to let families lead, and be integrated into processes as well. While they may be small, each positive impact that you have on the families in your community helps move the needle for child outcomes—and that is everyone's success.

Think beyond those families with whom you most frequently engage, and widen the scope of voices in the room. Who are the families and staff you rarely hear from? They will have the best advice for engaging others like themselves.

Once you have information about what success looks like in your setting, share it! Families and staff will let you know if you are hitting the mark. You will find out where you are already doing good work, and see what lessons you can apply to other areas.

Investing time in talking about outcomes

As you move forward and begin to build strategies into your framework, you might be overwhelmed by the lack of clarity about how to measure outcomes. Because family engagement is so broad, the outcomes can be hard to narrow. This is a challenge, but it also opens up opportunities to be creative in measuring how family engagement efforts directly impact your community.

Whatever your outcomes are, your plans for reaching these outcomes will, and should, change over time as you move through the process of learning and exploring how your families and community intersect. As you learn what truly matters to your community, you may identify new or different outcomes for your organization to share, and others for your partners to celebrate internally. This ebb and flow is natural when working towards a process of integrating engagement and partnership.

Values self-evaluation exercise

Throughout the book, you have been given opportunities to reflect on how your organization is strong in, or struggles with, each of the values. This piece-by-piece view of the values makes it feel much cleaner than it actually is. What you have seen demonstrated in these chapters is that these values do not exist in isolation, nor do they stay neatly in their own lanes. Even when you focus on one, the others are not static. This interdependence of the values adds to the complexity of family engagement work.

At the end of this book you will find the questions located at the end of each chapter complied into one resource. This self-evaluation exercise will guide you and your organization as you think about this complexity. Notice which values, or which pieces of the values, feel strongest. Consider how you might support gaps in other values by using strengths, or by shifting the way you are thinking about a particular topic or experience. Consider, too, how this self-evaluation might support you as an individual, or as an organization.

Using this book

We encourage you to use this book to spark conversations about where these values and your outcomes intersect, and to return to these conversations over time.

Each chapter in this book has highlighted the intentional effort needed to create lasting partnerships with families, based on a foundation of shared values. We hope reading it has helped to illuminate the many ways in which your organization can think about engaging families, and driving outcomes for children in a positive direction.

We set out to create a resource that helps you weave family engagement principles and practices into your work, in both large and small interactions. We've shared stories from the field, research-based strategies, and examples of state and national-level initiatives to remind you that a broader community is doing this work all around you. It's important to refresh your perspective from time to time by tapping into the collective energy generated by your peers, locally and nationally, who are also thinking and talking about family engagement. Their numbers are large, and growing by the day.

Thank you!

Each of you brings your own values, unique contributions, and ways of thinking to this work. We know this because we've heard from hundreds of people just like you. We've learned so much more than we have room to share in these pages. We hope you use this book as a springboard to propel your work even deeper, and to lay a foundation for sustainable practices.

The things you do each and every day are a part of your approach to family engagement. Your experiences and your knowledge of the community are invaluable. As you put the pieces together, you may find that there's something you want to share with us—and your words might just be a missing link for someone else. Please feel free to share your thoughts with us at Parents as Teachers (familyengagement@parentsasteachers.org). We'd love to hear about how you are pushing the work forward in home visiting, childcare centers, and schools.

Intentional partnerships are both challenging and incredibly rewarding when they fall into place. We wish you the best of luck on your engagement journey.

Values Self-Evaluation Exercise

Genuine relationships between organizations, families, and communities help kids thrive. Getting these ongoing partnerships started takes communication and commitment around shared values—and it is hard work. Once they're in place, they can be transformative!

Parents as Teachers offers these 10 values as a starting point for conversation as your family engagement partnerships unfold. Reflect on where you are on each one.

1. Trust

Trust forms the basis of solid relationships. Once trust is established, we can really go after our vision and goals together—and handle the inevitable challenges along the way.

□ We're strong on this.   □ We're so-so at this.   □ We're working on it.

2. Respect

Respecting each others' strengths, skills, knowledge, expertise, and experiences helps us start from a position of positive assumptions and empowerment.

□ We're strong on this.   □ We're so-so at this.   □ We're working on it.

3. Responsibility

Responsibility happens at both a personal and an organizational level. It includes stewardship of resources, following through on commitments, showing integrity, and holding others' best interest in mind.

□ We're strong on this.   □ We're so-so at this.   □ We're working on it.

4. Generosity

When generosity infuses partnerships, there is a spirit of sharing—whether it's time, resources, information, power, or authority.

☐ We're strong on this.   ☐ We're so-so at this.   ☐ We're working on it.

5. Accessibility

Extending an invitation is great, but it's important to consider accessibility. If everyone is ready, willing, and able to participate, they are more likely to accept the invitation.

☐ We're strong on this.   ☐ We're so-so at this.   ☐ We're working on it.

6. Integration

Within collective action, a deep level of commitment is required to acknowledge and utilize each individual child and adult, and recognize their contribution to the whole.

☐ We're strong on this.   ☐ We're so-so at this.   ☐ We're working on it.

7. Compassion

Compassion is easy to recognize when we experience it—through large or small examples of empathy, emotional connection, equitable treatment, perspective taking, or simply a warm welcome to a new situation.

☐ We're strong on this.   ☐ We're so-so at this.   ☐ We're working on it.

8. Initiative

Transformation needs a starting point. Taking the initiative means listening and learning from the community about where to start. We bring our best creative thinking to the table.

☐ We're strong on this.   ☐ We're so-so at this.   ☐ We're working on it.

9. Persistence

Transformation is hard work. It takes time for changes to become established, for setbacks to be overcome, and for those who are steadfast to be seen as assets.

☐ We're strong on this.　　☐ We're so-so at this.　　☐ We're working on it.

10. Sustainability

Once we put in the work to get something going, we want it to be around for a while. Sustainability means always keeping the goal in mind: to build lasting partnerships.

☐ We're strong on this.　　☐ We're so-so at this.　　☐ We're working on it.

Reflect and think ahead

Take a moment to reflect on your evaluation of these values. Which values are you or your organization strong in? Which are you still working on? Remember that engagement—including your feelings about how you are doing with each of these values—might vary based on a given time or context.

Use this evaluation to focus your efforts. How can you strengthen the values you marked as"so-so" or "working on"? Which values did you mark as "strong" that you want to continue to build on?

Take this opportunity to set goals around where you would like to see movement in the values, and check back in to see how you are doing every few weeks, months, or annually.

Notes

Introduction:

page 9 **Merriam-Webster defines family:** Family. (n.d.). *Merriam-Webster's online dictionary*. Retrieved from https://www.merriam-webster.com/dictionary/family

page 10 **perhaps the most well-known framework:** Mapp, K. & Kuttner, P. (2013). *Partners in education: A dual capacity-building framework for family-school partnerships*. SEDL in collaboration with the U.S. Department of Education. Retrieved from http://www.sedl.org/pubs/framework/FE-Cap-Building.pdf

page 10 **an update was published to the original definition:** Mapp, K., & Henderson, A. T. (2018, May 14). *State of family engagement: A conversation with Karen Mapp and Anne Henderson* [Webinar]. Hosted by the National Association for Family, School, and Community Engagement.

page 10 **there are many other definitions and frameworks for family engagement:** National Association for Family, School, and Community Engagement. (2010). *Family engagement defined*. Retrieved from https://nafsce.org/page/definition; Department of Health and Human Services, Administration for Children and Families, Children's Bureau, & Child Welfare Information Gateway. (n.d.). *Definitions of family engagement*. Retrieved from https://www.childwelfare.gov/fei/definition/; Engelman, K. (2017). *Family engagement: what is it and what does it look like?* Retrieved from ChildCare Aware of America website https://usa.childcareaware.org/2017/10/family-engagement-look-like/

page 10 **depict this continuum's defining characteristics:** Henderson, A. T., & Dahm, B. (2013, Nov. 5). *The pathway from fortress school to partnership school*. Retrieved from Education Week website www.edweek.org.

page 11 **a growing body of research that demonstrates all kinds of positive outcomes:** Headstart Early Childhood Learning and Knowledge Center. (2018). *Understanding family engagement outcomes: research to practice series*. Retrieved from https://eclkc.ohs.acf.hhs.gov/family-engagement/article/understanding-family-engagement-outcomes-research-practice-series; Department of Health and Human Services, Administration for Children and Families, Children's Bureau, & Child Welfare Information Gateway. (n.d). *Benefits of family engagement*. Retrieved from https://www.childwelfare.gov/FEI/benefits; Mapp, K. L., Carver, I. & Lander, J. (2017) *Powerful partnerships: A teacher's guide to engaging families for student success*. Scholastic, Inc. Retrieved from https://www.childwelfare.gov/FEI/benefits

page 11 **positive gains in many other areas as well:** Keyser, J. (2017). *From parents to partners: Building a family-centered early childhood program*. St. Paul, MN: Redleaf.

page 12 **"Since the U.S. Department of Education":** Panorama Education. (n.d.). *Reducing barriers to family engagement: How your district can understand and address common barriers to engagement with families* [White paper]. Retrieved from https://go.panoramaed.com/whitepaper/reducing-barriers-to-family-engagement.

page 12 **divides benefits to families:** Franklin, M. (2018, Jan. 11). *Ripples of transformation: Families leading change in early childhood system* [Webinar]. Hosted by First 5 Alameda County.

page 12 **they begin to attend events that increase their exposure:** U.S. Department of Health and Human Services, Administration for Children and Families, Children's Bureau, & Child Welfare Information Gateway. (2017). *Family engagement inventory: Commonalities across the benefits domain.* Retrieved from www.childwelfare.gov/FEI/benefits/

page 13 **parents empowered through engagement efforts are drawn to civic action:** Henderson, A. T., Kressley, K. G., & Frankel, S. (2016). *Capturing the ripple effect: Developing a theory of change for evaluating parent leadership initiatives (Final Report Phase 1).* Retrieved from Annenberg Institute website www.annenberginstitute.org/publications/capturing-ripple-effect

page 13 **The United Parent Leaders Action Network, or UPLAN:** United Parent Leaders Action Network. (n.d.). *Investing in parent leadership.* Retrieved from https://unitedparentleaders.org/our-work/

page 13 **higher morale, deeper understanding:** U.S. Department of Health and Human Services, Administration for Children and Families, Children's Bureau, & Child Welfare Information Gateway. (2017). *Family engagement inventory: Commonalities across the benefits domain.* Retrieved from www.childwelfare.gov/FEI/benefits/

page 13 **outcomes at the organizational level:** Forry, N., Moodie, S., Simkin, S., & Rothenberg, L. (2011). *Family-provider relationships: A multidisciplinary review of high quality practices and associations with family, child, and provider outcomes.* Retrieved from the Administration for Children and Families website www.acf.hhs.gov/programs/opre/resource/family-provider-relationships-a-multidisciplinary-review-of-high-quality

page 14 **a strong link between family engagement practices:** U.S. Department of Health and Human Services, Administration for Children and Families, Children's Bureau, & Child Welfare Information Gateway. (2017). *Family engagement inventory: Commonalities across the benefits domain.* Retrieved from www.childwelfare.gov/FEI/benefits/

page 14 **parent advocates can raise awareness:** Henderson, A. T., Kressley, K. G., & Frankel, S. (2016). *Capturing the ripple effect: Developing a theory of change for evaluating parent leadership initiatives (Final Report Phase 1).* Retrieved from www.annenberginstitute.org/publications/capturing-ripple-effect

page 17 **deserves to be recognized:** Center for the Study of Social Policy. (n.d.) *Strengthening Families: Increasing positive outcomes for children and families.* Retrieved from https://cssp.org/our-work/project/strengthening-families/

page 18 **"policies, practice methods,":** National Technical Assistance and Evaluation Center for Systems of Care. (2008). *An individualized, strengths-based approach in public child welfare driven systems of care.* Retrieved from *Child Welfare Information Gateway website* https://www.childwelfare.gov/pubs/acloserlook/strengthsbased/strengthsbased1/

page 19 **"negativity bias":** Baumeister, R.F., Bratslavsky, E., Finkenauer, C., & Vohs, K.D. (2001). Bad is Stronger Than Good. *General Review of Psychology, 5, (4)* 323-370. doi: 10.1037//1089-2680.5.4.323

page 19 **equipping everyone to influence decisions:** Bandura, A. (1977). Self-efficacy: Toward a unifying theory of behavioral change. *Psychological Review, 84(2),* 191-215; Zimmerman, M. A. (1995). Psychological empowerment: Issues and illustrations. *American Journal of Community Psychology, 23(5),* 581-599; and Zimmerman, M. A., & Warschausky, S. (1998). Empowerment theory for rehabilitation research: Conceptual and methodological issues. *Rehabilitation Psychology, 43,* 316.

page 19 **"Families are children's first and most important teachers"**: U.S. Department of Health and Human Services & U.S. Department of Education. (2016). *Policy statement on family engagement: From the early years to the early grades.* Retrieved from www2.ed.gov/about/inits/ ed/earlylearning/files/policy-statement-on-family-engagement.pdf

page 20 **the most critical components of family engagement**: Roggman, L. A., Boyce, L. K., & Innocenti, M. S. (2008). *Developmental parenting: A guide for early childhood practitioners.* Baltimore: Paul H. Brookes.

page 21 **"In too many cases"**: Pekel, K., Roehlkepartain, E.C., Syvertsen, A.K., & Scales, P.C. (2015). *Don't forget the families: The missing piece in America's effort to help all children succeed.* Minneapolis, MN: Search Institute.

page 21 **support, but not replace parents' own goals**: Katz, L. (1995). *Talks with teachers of young children: A collection.* Norwood, NJ: Ablex.

Chapter 1: Trust

page 25 **it could take three times as long**: Roehlpartain, E. C. (2018, May 1). *Stop 'recruiting' parents (and what to do instead).* [Live webinar]. Search Institute.

page 25 **"Trust is built over time"**: Garcia, M. E., Frunzi, K., Dean, C. B., Flores, N., & Miller, K. B. (2016). *Toolkit of resources for engaging families and the community as partners in education – part 3: Building trusting relationships with families and the community through effective communication.* Denver, CO: Regional Educational Laboratory Pacific. Retrieved from the Institute of Education Sciences website https://ies.ed.gov/ncee/edlabs/projects/project. asp?projectID=4509

page 26 **"That is where I get the most valuable feedback"**: Parents as Teachers & Strong Fathers-Strong Families (Producers). (2018, June 26). Engage In: Accessibility. *Intentional Partnerships.* [Audio podcast]. Retrieved from http://intentionalpartnerships.libsyn.com/engage-inaccessibilty

page 26 **five key components that are necessary for building trust**: Tschannen-Moran, M. (2014). *Trust matters: Leadership for successful school* (2nd ed.). San Francisco, CA: Jossey-Bass.

page 27 **"within an early childhood program"**: Parents as Teachers & Strong Fathers-Strong Families (Producers). (2018, July 10). Engage In: Compassion. *Intentional Partnerships* [Audio podcast]. Retrieved from http://intentionalpartnerships.libsyn.com/engage-in-compassion

page 28 **just a structure with possibility**: Ishimaru, A. M. (2014). When new relationships meet old narrative: The journey towards improving parent-school relations in a district-community organizing collaborative. *Teachers College Record, 116 (2)* 1-49.

page 29 **more willing to trust the organization or school**: Fullan, M. (2011). *Choosing the wrong drivers for educational reform.* Centre for Strategic Education Seminar Series. East Melbourne, Victoria; Kaplan Early Learning Company. (2019). *Developing Trust and Nourishing Respect in the Classroom.* Retrieved from https://www.kaplanco.com/ii/developing-trust-nourishing-respect

page 30 **something they value (such as their child!)**: Feltman, C. (2008). *The thin book of trust: An essential primer for building trust at work.* Bend, OR: Thin Book.

page 30 **"A focus on relationship building"**: Mapp, K. & Kuttner, P. (2013). *Partners in education: A dual capacity-building framework for family-school partnerships.* SEDL in collaboration with the U.S. Department of Education. Retrieved from http://www.sedl.org/pubs/framework/FE-Cap-Building.pdf

page 32 **transforming a disagreement**: Brown, B. (2017). *Braving the wilderness: The quest for true belonging and the courage to stand alone.* New York: Random House.

page 33 **"Rebuilding trust requires a consistent and dependable energy"**: Horsmon, S. (2017, March 6). *How to avoid the pursuer-distancer pattern in your relationship* [Blog post]. Retrieved from The Gottman Institute website www.gottman.com/blog/how-to-avoid-the-pursuer-distancer-pattern-in-your-relationship

page 34 **"Trust promotes dialogue"**: Student Achievement Division. (2012). *Ontario Capacity Building Series K-12. Secretariat Special Edition #29.* Retrieved from http://edu.gov.on.ca/eng/literacynumeracy/inspire/research/CBS_parentEngage.pd

page 35 **The structure of the café supports initial dialogue**: Center for the Study of Social Policy. (2014). *Using café conversations to build protective factors and parent leadership.* Retrieved from www.cssp.org/reform/strengtheningfamilies/2014/USING-CAF-CONVERSATIONS-TO-BUILD-PROTECTIVE-FACTORS-AND-PARENT-LEADERSHIP.pdf

page 35 **Look to Strengthening Families for more information on their Parent Cafés**: Center for the Study of Social Policy (2015). *Using café conversations to build protective factors and parent leadership.* Retrieved from https://cssp.org/resource/cafe-overview-2015/

page 35 **This model is derived from the World Café model, via *Zero to Three***: Zero to Three. (2016). *Caring conversations café model facilitator guide.* Retrieved from https://www.zerotothree.org/resources/657-caring-conversations-cafe-model-facilitator-guide

page 35 **The Right Question Institute teaches the skill of asking good questions**: Right Question Institute. (2019). *Build effective school-family partnerships.* Retrieved from https://rightquestion.org/schools-families/

page 39 **"consistent and positive communication"**: U.S. Department of Health and Human Services & U.S. Department of Education. (n.d.) *Policy statement on family engagement from the early years to the early grades.* Retrieved from https://www.acf.hhs.gov/sites/default/files/ecd/draft_hhs_ed_family_engagement.pdf

page 42 **when families and schools trust each other**: Bryk, A.S., Sebring, P.B., Allensworth, E., Luppescu, S., & Easton, J.Q. (2009). Organizing schools for improvement: lessons from Chicago. Retrieved from https://www.press.uchicago.edu/ucp/books/book/chicago/O/bo8212979.html; Case, M. & Davidson, K. L. (2018) *Building trust, elevating voices, and sharing power in family partnership.* Retrieved from Phi Delta Kappan website https://www.kappanonline.org/davidson-building-trust-elevating-voices-sharing-power-family-partnership/

page 44 **"to share experiences and information."** Normandy Schools Collaborative (n.d.). *Strengthen systems: Leadership and facilitation bring about systems change.* Retrieved from https://www.normandysc.org/Page/1352

Chapter 2: Respect

page 47 **"respect for others"**: Student Achievement Division. (2012). *Ontario Capacity Building Series K-12. Secretariat Special Edition #29.* Retrieved from http://edu.gov.on.ca/eng/literacynumeracy/inspire/research/CBS_parentEngage.pdf

page 48 **appreciation, acceptance, and respect**: Semmer, N. K., Meier, L. L., & Beehr, T. A. (2016). Social aspects of work: Direct and indirect social messages conveying respect or disrespect. In A. M. Rossi, J. A. Meurs, & P. L. Perrewé (Eds.). *Stress and quality of working life: Interpersonal and occupation-based stress* (pp. 13-31). Charlotte, NC, US: IAP Information Age.

page 49 **grade-level outcomes for Physical Education**: SHAPE America. (2013). *Grade-level outcomes for K-12 physical education.* Reston, VA: Author.

Page 51 **"the more parents perceive teachers as valuing their contributions"**: State Advisory Council for Parent Involvement in Education. (2019). *Family, school, and community partnering research to practice: doing what works!* Colorado Department of Education. Retrieved from https://www.cde.state.co.us/sacpie

page 53 **face-to-face conversations:** Roehlpartain, E. C. (2018, May 1). *Stop 'recruiting' parents (and what to do instead).* [Live webinar]. Search Institute.

page 61 **When families are respected they can feel it:** Larson, Sandra. (2018, July 24). Together, parents boost their children's early learning. *The New York Times.* Retrieved from: https://www.nytimes.com/2018/07/24/opinion/early-learning-boston-parenting.html

page 61 **"Language matters":** Ibid

page 62 **"I think that we have to remember":** Parents as Teachers & Strong Fathers-Strong Families (Producers). (2018, July 10). Engage In: Compassion. *Intentional Partnerships* [Audio podcast]. Retrieved from http://intentionalpartnerships.libsyn.com/engage-in-compassion

page 63 **our own backgrounds influence our expectations:** Tanner, D. (1990). *You just don't understand: Women and men in conversation* (pp. 93-99). New York, NY: Morrow.

page 64 **"It is the goal":** U.S. Department of Health and Human Services & U.S. Department of Education. (2016). *Policy statement on family engagement: From the early years to the early grades.* Retrieved from www2.ed.gov/about/inits/ed/earlylearning/files/policy-statement-on-family-engagement.pdf

page 65 **"The NCPFCE [National Center on Parent, Family, and Community Engagement]":** Engelman, K. (2017). *Family engagement: what is it and what does it look like?* Retrieved from ChildCare Aware of America website https://usa.childcareaware.org/2017/10/family-engagement-look-like/

page 68 **empowering parents with knowledge:** Garcia, M. E., Frunzi, K. Dean, C. B., Flores, N., & Miller, K. (2016). *Toolkit of resources for engaging families and the community and partners in education, Part 4: Engaging all in data conversations* (REL 2016-153). Washington, DC: U.S. Department of Education, Institute of Education Sciences, National Center for Education Evaluation and Regional Assistance, Regional Educational Laboratory Pacific. Retrieved from Institute of Education Services website https://ies.ed.gov/ncee/edlabs/projects/project.asp?projectID=4509

Chapter 3: Responsibility

page 74 **The phrase "shared responsibility":** Global Family Research Project. (2018). *Leading family engagement in early learning: A supplemental guide* [Research publication]. Retrieved from https://globalfrp.org/Articles/Leading-Family-Engagement-in-Early-Learning-A-Supplemental-Guide; U.S. Department of Health and Human Services, Administration for Children and Families, & National Center on Parent, & Family, and Community Engagement. (n.d.). *Parent involvement and family engagement for early childhood professionals.* Retrieved from https://eclkc.ohs.acf.hhs.gov/sites/default/files/pdf/parent-involvement-family-engagement-for-professionals.pdf; Ferlazzo, L. (2016, Jan. 26). *Response: 'Successful schools solicit' family engagement* [Blog post]. Retrieved April 26, 2019, from https://blogs.edweek.org/teachers/classroom_qa_with_larry_ferlazzo/2016/01/response_successful_schools_solicit_family_engagement.html; Crew, R., & Dyja, T. (2007). *Only connect: The way to save our schools.* New York: Farrar, Straus, and Giroux

page 76 **strong parallels here:** Weisberg, D. S., Hirsh-Pasek, K., Golinkoff, R. M., & McCandliss, B. D. (2014). Mise en place: Setting the stage for thought and action. *Trends in Cognitive Sciences, 18 (6),* 276-279. doi: 10.1016/j.tics.2014

page 78 **such as setting and respecting boundaries:** Wachter, H. (2018, Dec.). Why trust matters—and how to build more of it. *Experience Life.* Retrieved from https://experiencelife.com/article/why-trust-matters-and-how-to-build-more-of-it/

page 79 **as the school's reputation:** Parents as Teachers & Strong Fathers-Strong Families (Producers). (2018, Oct. 17). Engage In: Compassion Part 2. *Intentional Partnerships* [Audio podcast]. Retrieved from https://parentsasteachers.org/intentional-partnerships-podcast-blog/2018/10/17/engage-in-compassion-part-ii

page 83 **it can be beneficial to lay them out:** Parents as Teachers National Center. (2018). *Facilitating groups* [Training]. St. Louis, MO: Author.

page 83 **a policy that lays out what the board, district, and schools:** Portland Board of Public Education. (n.d.). *School and family partnership policy.* Retrieved from https://usm.maine.edu/sites/default/files/eems/School%20Partner%20Policy.pdf

page 84 **highlighting positive experiences and moments of growth can go a long way:** Westmoreland, H., Rosenberg, H. M., Lopez, M. E., & Weiss, H. (2009). *Seeing is believing: Promising practices for how school districts promote family engagement* [Issue brief]. Retrieved April 26, 2019, from https://archive.globalfrp.org/publications-resources/browse-our-publications/seeing-is-believing-promising-practices-for-how-school-districts-promote-family-engagement

page 86 **"If anxiety and mistrust can prevent families":** Successful Innovations, Inc. (n.d.). *A correlation/crosswalk of family engagement on demand to the dual capacity building framework.* Retrieved from https://static1.squarespace.com/static/58f6ec52ff7c5042d6755351/t/5914fa cac534a532e2a78ad9/1494547147734/Crosswalk+Dual+Capacity+Platform+eBook.pdf

page 87 **it comes in the form of conversations and qualitative data collection:** Tredway, L. (2018, July 11). *Metrics that make sense: Using our stories to demonstrate impact.* Presentation at the Institute for Educational Leadership conference, Cleveland, OH.

page 87 **formalized processes for gathering feedback:** Militello, M., Janson, C., Guajardo, F., & Guajardo, M. A. (2019, Jan.). Mobilize the power of CLEs: Don't leave community learning exchanges behind. *Principal Leadership.* Retrieved from the National Association of Secondary School Principals website www.nassp.org/2019/01/01/mobilize-the-power-of-cles/

Chapter 4: Generosity

page 95 **professionals sometimes view families:** Pekel, K., Roehlkepartain, E. G., Syvertsen, A. K., & Scales, P. C. (2015). *Don't forget the families: The missing piece in America's effort to help all children succeed.* Minneapolis, MN: Search Institute.

Page 100 **A structured way to give input on decisions and direction:** Rowland, A. (2016, July 26). *Three lessons in developing a systemic approach to family engagement* [Blog post]. Retrieved July 26, 2016, from the Harvard Family Research Project website www.hfrp.org/hfrp-news/blog-new-directions-in-family-engagement/three-lessons-in-developing-a-systemic-approach-to-family-engagement

Page 102 **strategies that are implemented across an entire community can be very impactful:** Intercultural Development Research Association. (2018). *Learn more about IDRA's Education CAFÉ model.* Retrieved from www.idra.org/families-and-communities/learn-more-about-idras-education-cafe-model/; National League of Cities. (2016). *Issue brief: Creating local early education systems that support healthy child development and thriving communities.* Retrieved from www.nlc.org/resource/educational-alignment-for-young-children; Portland Empowered. (n.d.). *Parent engagement partners.* Retrieved from www.portlandempowered.org/parent-engagement-partners

Page 103 **part of its** *Interactive rubric*: Boston Public Schools Focus on Children. (2008). *What is the Interactive Rubric?* Retrieved from https://www.bostonpublicschools.org/site/Default.aspx?PageID=531

Chapter 5: Accessibility

page 107 **"Obviously, as we all know":** Parents as Teachers & Strong Fathers-Strong Families (Producers). (2018, June 26). Engage In: Accessibility. *Intentional Partnerships.* [Audio podcast]. Retrieved from http://intentionalpartnerships.libsyn.com/engage-inaccessibilty

page 108 **"we look at best practices":** Ibid

page 110 **Americans with Disabilities Act (ADA) Compliance:** United States Department of Justice Civil Rights Division. (n.d.) *Information and Technical Assistance on the Americans with Disabilities Act.* Retrieved from https://www.ada.gov/

page 118 **More than 4.4 million U.S. students are learning English at school as a second language:** U.S. Department of Education, National Center for Education Statistics. (2014). *The condition of education 2014* (NCES Fast Facts No. 2014-083). Retrieved April 27, 2015, from http://nces.ed.gov/pubs2014.

page 121 **"If I am a gatekeeper":** Parents as Teachers & Strong Fathers-Strong Families (Producers). (2018, July 10). Engage In: Compassion. *Intentional Partnerships* [Audio podcast]. Retrieved from http://intentionalpartnerships.libsyn.com/engage-in-compassion

page 125 **these power differences can be real or perceived:** Heijes, C. (2011). Cross-cultural perception and power dynamics across changing organizational and national contexts: Curaçao and the Netherlands. *Human Relations, 64 (5),* 653–674. https://doi.org/10.1177/0018726710386394

Chapter 6: Integration

page 130 **"allowing things to be different or distinct from each other":** Siegel, D. (2018). *Aware: The science and practice of presence.* New York: Tarcher Perigree/Penguin Random House.

Page 131 **we are not even aware of the multitude of social and cultural contexts:** Parents as Teachers National Center. (2018). *Diversity in families, children and you* [online training]. St. Louis, MO: Author.

page 132 **well-intentioned programs:** Carter, M. (2015). *Redefining parent engagement: An interview with Mary Jo Deck.* Retrieved from Childcare Exchange website https://facweb.northseattle.edu/bwilli/ParentEdInstructorResources/Parent%20Educator%20Handbook/Redefining%20Parent%20Engagement_PV.pdf

page 132 **individuals photograph their day:** Wang, C., & Burris, M. A. (1997). Photovoice: Concept, Methodology and Use for Participatory Needs Assessment. *Health Education and Behavior, 24(3),* 369-387. doi: 10.1177/109019819702400309.

page 135 **tend to be involved in a more hands-on way:** Antony-Newman, M. (2016, Nov. 30). School demands for parents to do more hits low-income and minority students hardest. *The Conversation.* Retrieved from https://theconversation.com/school-demands-for-parents-to-do-more-hits-low-income-and-minority-students-hardest-67068

page 137 **characteristics that indicate family strengths:** Search Institute. (2012). *Family assets.* Retrieved from www.search-institute.org/wp-content/uploads/2018/02/Family_Assets_Framework.pdf.; DeFrain, J., & Asay, S. (2013). *Strong families around the world: Strengths-based research and perspectives.* New York: Routledge. doi: 10.4324/9780203726273; Center for the Study of Social Policy. (2018). *Core meanings of the strengthening families protective factors.* Retrieved from https://cssp.org/wp-content/uploads/2018/10/Core-Meanings-of-the-SF-Protective-Factors-2015.pdf

page 138 **The Gente Puente ("bridge builders") podcast:** Patti's Catholic Corner. (Producer). (n.d.). *Connect with Hispanics.* [Audio podcast] Retrieved from http://patticc.com/gentepuente/

page 139 **the importance of filling in gaps in knowledge:** Condliffe, B. F., Boyd, M. L., & DeLuca, S. (2015). Stuck in school: how social context shapes school choice for inner-city students. *Teachers College Record, 117(3),* 1-36.

page 140 **cultural models:** Pineau, M. G. (2017). *Immigration, safety and security: Framing data to tell a better story* [webinar]. Retrieved Oct. 19, 2017, from www.youtube.com/watch?v=4cOA79slH14

Page 141 **food can be a shared experience:** National Association for Family, School and Community Engagement. (2018, July 12). Group discussion at the Institute for Education Leadership National Conference. Cleveland, OH; Gomez-Mont, G. (2019, Jan. 15). *Creativity unbound: The need for urban experimentation.* COCAbiz presentation at Innovation Hall, St. Louis, MO.

page 149 **the impact of collective assembly:** Brown, B. (2017). *Braving the wilderness: The quest for true belonging and the courage to stand alone.* New York: Random House.

page 150 **"[w]e're going to need":** Brown, B. (2017). *Braving the wilderness: The quest for true belonging and the courage to stand alone* (pp. 37). New York: Random House.

Chapter 7: Compassion

page 153 **Humans are hardwired to empathize:** Cook, Gareth. (2013). Why we are wired to connect. *Scientific American.* Retrieved from https://www.scientificamerican.com/article/why-we-are-wired-to-connect/?redirect=1

page 153 **"sympathetic consciousness of others' distress together with a desire to alleviate it":** Compassion. (n.d.). *Merriam-Webster's online dictionary.* Retrieved from https://www.merriam-webster.com/dictionary/compassion

page 155 **how our brains react to empathy and compassion:** Well, Tara. (2017). Compassion is better than empathy. *Psychology Today.* Retreived from https://www.psychologytoday.com/us/blog/the-clarity/201703/compassion-is-better-empathy

page 156 **"The competent aspect of social work ":** Swindell, M. L. (2014). Compassionate Competence: A New Model for Social Work Practice. *The New Social Worker.* Retrieved from https://www.socialworker.com/feature-articles/practice/compassionate-competence-a-new-model-for-social-work-practi/

page 157 **increasing compassion is not only possible:** Weng, H. Y., Fox, A. S., Shackman, A. J., Stodola, D. E., Caldwell, J. Z. K., Olson, M. C., ... Davidson, R. J. (2013). Compassion Training Alters Altruism and Neural Responses to Suffering. *Psychological Science, 24 (7),* 1171–1180. https://doi.org/10.1177/0956797612469537

page 159 **to deepen our compassionate practices to include:** Greater Good Science Center at the University of California, Berkeley. (2019). Compassion: how do I cultivate it? *Greater Good Magazine.* Retrieved from https://greatergood.berkeley.edu/topic/compassion/definition#how-cultivate-compassion

page 159 **differences in brain activity after experiencing compassion:** Well, Tara. (2017) Compassion is better than empathy. *Psychology Today.* Retreived from https://www.psychologytoday.com/us/blog/the-clarity/201703/compassion-is-better-empathy

page 160 **compassionate care not only feels:** Fotaki, M. (2015). Why and how is compassion necessary to provide good quality healthcare? *International Journal of Health Policy Management (4),* 199–201. doi: 10.15171/ijhpm.2015.66

page 160 **leads to speedier recoveries:** Ibid

page 160 **local governments and schools around the world:** Parent Map. (2012). *Teaching compassion: Changing the world through empathy and education.* Retrieved from https://www.parentmap.com/article/compassion-changing-the-world-through-empathy-and-education

page 160 **"to work tirelessly"**: Charter for Compassion. (n.d.). *Charter Overview* (para.1). Retrieved from https://charterforcompassion.org/charter/charter-overew

page 163 **"treating yourself with the same kindness"**: Wong, K. (2017, Dec. 28). Why self-compassion beats self-confidence. *The New York Times.* Retrieved from https://www.nytimes.com/2017/12/28/smarter-living/why-self-compassion-beats-self-confidence.html

page 164 **"We have to get really real"**: Parents as Teachers & Strong Fathers-Strong Families (Producers). (2018, July 10). Engage In: Compassion. *Intentional Partnerships* [Audio podcast]. Retrieved from http://intentionalpartnerships.libsyn.com/engage-in-compassion

page 165 **organizations cannot rely solely on individual practitioners'**: Fotaki, M. (2015). Why and how is compassion necessary to provide good quality healthcare? *International Journal of Health Policy Management (4)*, 199–201. doi: 10.15171/ijhpm.2015.66/

Chapter 8: Initiative

page 174 **"Human-centered design isn't a perfectly linear process"**: IDEO.org. (2015). *The Field Guide to Human-Centered Design* (pp. 11). Canada: IDEO.org.

page 174 **"Human-centered design offers"**: IDEO.org. (2015). *The Field Guide to Human-Centered Design.* (pp 9). Canada: IDEO.org.

page 175 **a "co-design" approach**: Haight, S., Abdulle, F., Chan, R., & Paananen, K. K. (2018, Sept. 27). *What is 2 gen? Exploring the 2 gen approach to family engagement and why it works* [Live webinar]. Ascend at the Aspen Institute.

page 177 **conversations that seek common ground**: Brown, B. (2017). *Braving the wilderness: The quest for true belonging and the courage to stand alone.* New York: Random House

page 179 **develop an early childhood education culture**: Geller, J. (2017, June 6). *Connecting a village: How does the i3 'We are a village' grant enhance social capital?* [Live webinar]. Hosted by the National Association for Family, School, and Community Engagement, National Coalition for Parent Involvement in Education, & Investing in Innovation Fund.

page 180 *Strong Fathers-Strong Families*: website https://www.strongfathers.com/

page 180 **her approach to the job was informed**: Parents as Teachers & Strong Fathers-Strong Families (Producers). (2018, Sept. 18). Engage In: Initiative. *Intentional Partnerships.* [Audio podcast]. Retrieved from https://parentsasteachers.org/intentional-partnerships-podcast-blog/2018/9/18/intentional-partnerships-podcast-episode-7-engage-in-initiative.

Chapter 9: Persistence

page 185 **Karla Kush calls these "2-by-10 kids."**: Parents as Teachers & Strong Fathers Strong Families (Producers). (2018, Sept. 18). Engage In: Initiative. *Intentional Partnerships.* [Audio podcast]. Retrieved from https://parentsasteachers.org/intentional-partnerships-podcast-blog/2018/9/18/intentional-partnerships-podcast-episode-7-engage-in-initiative.

page 186 **"unable to show whether such a program"**: Smetzer-Anderson, S., Roessler, J., & Kratochwill, T. R. (2018). *Inroads in family engagement in urban elementary schools: Lessons learned in the Investing in Family Engagement Project, 2013-2018.* Retrieved from the Wisconsin Center for Education Research website http://phillyfasti3.wceruw.org/assets/Lessons-learned-report.pdf.

page 187 **"[T]he lessons we learned over five years"**: Ibid

page 187 **strong collaborative work by the implementation team**: Ibid

page 187 **family engagement as a process**: Caspe, M. (2015, Apr. 22). *Effective family engagement for transitions to school* [Webinar]. Hosted by National Association for Family, School and Community Engagement.

page 189 **"dropping out of school"**: America's Promise Alliance. (2016). *Overview and 4A framework*. Retrieved from www.americaspromise.org/overview-and-4a-framework

page 190 **experiences staff members have not had can be a barrier**: Parents as Teachers National Center. (2015). *Diversity in families, children and you*. St. Louis, MO: Author.

page 190 **"funds of knowledge"**: Shafer, L. (2018, Apr. 26). *Partnering with newcomer families* [Blog post]. Retrieved Nov. 20, 2018, from Harvard Graduate School of Education website www. gse.harvard.edu/news/uk/18/04/partnering-newcomer-families

page 191 **each interaction is a new opportunity**: Caspe, M. (2015, Apr. 22). *Effective family engagement for transitions to school* [Webinar]. Hosted by National Association for Family, School and Community Engagement.

page 192 **pathways may change as children get older**: Ibid.

page 192 **"A lot of times, parents don't hear that"**: Morton, N. (2017, Sept. 27). Harvard professor's quest: Persuade every teacher to build stronger ties with families. *The Seattle Times* (para. 16). Retrieved from www.seattletimes.com.

page 193 **the systematic identification of transition points**: Caspe, M. (2015, Apr. 22). *Effective family engagement for transitions to school* [Webinar]. Hosted by National Association for Family, School and Community Engagement.

Chapter 10: Sustainability

page 200 **offer detailed guidance**: Zeribi, K., Mackrain, M., Arbour, M., & O'Carroll, K. (2017). *Partnering with families in continuous quality improvement: The Maternal, Infant, and Early Childhood Home Visiting Program* (OPRE Report #2017-47). Washington, DC: Office of Planning, Research and Evaluation, U.S. Department of Health and Human Services.

page 201 **implies people will only contribute or participate productively**: Ryan, J. (2018, Dec. 5). Life Work Systems. *Your extraordinary workplace* [Webinar]. Retrieved Jan. 14, 2019, from www. youtube.com/watch?v=sqNA7xqSMyU&feature=youtube.

Page 207 **adult learning theory states**: Zoller, K. & Landry, C. (2010). *The Choreography of Presenting: The 7 Essential Abilities of Effective Presenters*. Thousand Oaks, CA: Corwin A SAGE Company.

Page 209 **many new sources of philanthropic funding**: Reilly, C. (2018, March 1). *Support by education funders for family engagement is growing. Why is that?* [Blog post]. Retrieved from Inside Philanthrophy website www.insidephilanthropy.com/home/2018/3/1/foundations-education-grants-family-engagement